IMAGES
of America

CINCINNATI
ON FIELD AND COURT

THE SPORTS LEGACY OF THE QUEEN CITY

Jack Twyman, one of the greatest basketball players in Cincinnati sports history, was an All-American at the University of Cincinnati before being signed by the NBA Rochester Royals in 1955. Two years later, the Royals relocated to the Queen City, and Twyman became a mainstay for the team. He was an All-Star for six of his eleven pro seasons, and in 1982 Twyman was elected to the National Basketball Hall of Fame.

IMAGES
of America

CINCINNATI
ON FIELD AND COURT

THE SPORTS LEGACY OF THE QUEEN CITY

Kevin Grace

ARCADIA
PUBLISHING

Published by Arcadia Publishing
Charleston, South Carolina

Library of Congress Catalog Card Number: 2002110397

For all general information contact Arcadia Publishing at:
Telephone 843-853-2070
Fax 843-853-0044
E-mail sales@arcadiapublishing.com
For customer service and orders:
Toll-Free 1-888-313-2665

Visit us on the Internet at www.arcadiapublishing.com

21—Crosley Field, Cincinnati, Ohio,
"Home of the Cincinnati Reds"

Crosley Field was the classic home of the Cincinnati Reds. Situated at the corner of Findlay
Street and Western Avenue on the site of an old brickyard in the West End, the ballpark had
its beginnings in 1884 as League Park. League Park gave way to the Palace of the Fans in 1902,
which was enlarged and reborn as Redland Field in 1912. In 1934, when Powel Crosley Jr.
bought the team, the name again was changed. After more than 80 years at this location, the
Reds moved to Riverfront Stadium in 1970.

CONTENTS

ACKNOWLEDGMENTS

Dedicated to all my students at the University of Cincinnati. Run hard, go for the extra base, and read forever.

Thank you to my UC colleagues: Greg Hand, Tom Hathaway, Don Heinrich Tolzmann, Anna Truman, Tom White, Jay Yocis, and especially Jerry Reid, for supporting my courses on sports and society.

Thanks, also, to Maggie Yax and the Cincinnati Historical Society, Jan Evans and the Wyoming (Ohio) Historical Society, the German Heritage Museum, Harry Talkers and Doris Wilke of the Catholic Kolping Society, Larry Herms and Erin Vernon of the Cincinnati Reds, Donn Burrows, Bob Clements, Stuart Hodesh, Dan Nathan, Jo Ann Pipes, Kevin Proffitt, and Jack Twyman.

Special acknowledgments are due to John Erardi and Lonnie Wheeler, two of the best sports journalists in Cincinnati history.

And, of course, appreciation to the home team: Joan, Josh, Sean, Courtney, Bonnie, and Lily.

INTRODUCTION

A baseball fable was published in Cincinnati in 1885 that captured the place of sports in the city. Titled "O'Toole's Ghost," the tale appeared anonymously in a local weekly tabloid that featured satirical cartoons and articles about life in Cincinnati and America. In the story, a young Irish delinquent by the name of Mickey McGonigle is anxious to become a star player for the Cincinnati ball team, and, in a dream, he is advised by the ghost of a dead pitcher, the outstanding Barney O'Toole, that success will come for him if he just remembers never to argue with the umpire. He will be the greatest ballplayer ever. Cincinnati is called "Sweinburg" in the story; the owner of the local "Dirty Stockings" club is German-Jewish; the umpire is hated; the crowd is made up of women, men, and children representing all social and economic classes; gambling is rife; and every Cincinnati ethnic stereotype imaginable is spun into the telling. Unfortunately, during a crucial moment of a game, McGonigle argues the umpire's call on a foul ball and thus loses his athletic talent as quickly as he acquired it. He is reduced to a life of pushing an ash-cart through the Cincinnati streets and muttering to himself. People look at him, point to their heads, and say, "a victim of the base ball craze."

In short, this one little story neatly encompasses every aspect of the 19th century city and professional sports. And, surprisingly, those aspects are little different from cities and sports more than a century later—race and ethnicity, economics, social issues like gambling, and celebrity worship.

It was the city in America that gave rise to organized sports. Without a resident population large enough in size, some disposable income (for attendance or gambling), and free time (such as it was; a result of the Industrial Revolution, with established work hours and wages), team sports and organized leisure activities would not have developed. There would be no spacious ballparks, no swimming pools, no basketball courts and boxing rings, no arenas and field houses and playgrounds. It is from the cities in the 19th and early 20th centuries that sports, as we know them today, spread to every corner of the country, making us a sports nation in the 21st century.

The reason why "O'Toole's Ghost" still resonates in the chamber of our collective sports memory is that the people, the setting, and the situations are still very familiar. We know ballplayers and owners like this today. We recognize the crowd at the ballpark, and can identify with the seemingly arbitrary decisions of an umpire. We feel the competition between one community and another. And, we feel the exhilaration that sports give to our everyday lives.

Cincinnati, like other 19th century Midwestern cities, was settled by people from the Middle Atlantic and eastern seaboard states, and by mid-century had a tremendous influx of European immigrants. Forming the new urban working class, these citizens gathered in groups with which they naturally had something in common: ethnicity, national origin, faith, or occupation. Males often bonded together in these similarities in what has come to be called the saloon, or bachelor, subculture.

In working class saloons, away from the gentlemanly expression of sport by the middle and upper classes, men drank, caroused, fought, and gambled over sporting propositions. Bloodsports and betting on them were the norm. These bloodsports—boxing, rat-baiting, cockfighting, or dog fighting—have always existed just beyond the pale of society, constantly debated in terms of morals and ethics. They existed then, and exist now, because of the element of the wager. In reaction, as early as 1843 a group called the United States Anti-Gambling and Moral Trust Society met in Cincinnati to draw up a constitution and organize their outrage against such activities.

At the same time, sports and athletic activity grew among the other segments of the population. Gymnastic clubs and shooting clubs were created. The YMCA movement combined physical fitness with moral and spiritual fitness, in part to battle the influence of the saloons. And, baseball continued to grow. With the professionalization of the game following the Civil War, the amateur, middle-class, gentleman players were replaced by those with working class origins who viewed sport as a path to economic respectability. College sports such as football developed, and urban leisure time was taken up with tennis, bowling, bicycling, skating, and walking. Competitive events were embraced even more by fans and athletes, and bloodsport would not disappear (as it never will in human affairs). This divergence of interests made the city a veritable world of athletics in every form, for every type of sports fan.

As America rushed into the 20th century, sport became king in Queen City. Entire sections of newspapers came to be devoted solely to the description, dissection and discussion of games and personalities. The Reds would win five World Series. Professional football—Celts, Redlegs, Blades, Bengals—would sputter and start, die out, and roar to life again. Bearcat and Musketeer college basketball would become the talk of the nation. The National Basketball Association would come and go, and so would championship boxers. The Flying Pig Marathon would attract runners from around the globe. And, there would be ballpark built upon ballpark, stadiums gracing the Ohio River, racetracks slotted here and there, and the filling of arenas and halls and "centers" and "gardens."

In the last decades of the 20th century and into this new millennium, sport also has flexed its considerable economic muscle, both nationally and locally. But just as important have been the other community sports of the city, complementing the professional teams from baseball and football to basketball and soccer: Special Olympics and Senior Olympics, tennis courts and golf courses, recreational baseball and softball, and neighborhood bowling teams. New examples of sport and community are the Oakley Cycle Club's race series in Cincinnati's Mt. Lookout Park and the Ohio River Run of kayaks and canoes to promote the ecological importance of the river. Both events hearken back to a century ago when competitive bicycle races were common and a score of canoe clubs existed in Cincinnati.

Sports provide us with a sense of place, and there are only two reasons for writing this book: understanding and appreciation.

Kevin Grace

One

BUILDING A CITY AND DEVELOPING SPORT

THE 19TH CENTURY

In 1884, the baseball squad became the first organized athletic team at the University of Cincinnati. The players donned whatever they thought would pass as uniforms and played against whatever local teams would give them a game. In 1886, the UC nine played its first intercollegiate game, against Miami University, winning 14–5. This photo of the 1894 team shows the UC players finally wearing identical uniforms, purchased as a result of a benefit game against the Reds the year before. The Reds beat the collegians 32–7.

In the years leading up to the Civil War, the sport of baseball was dominated by amateur clubs with the occasional paid ringer thrown in. America clung to the image of the game as a "gentleman's" activity, but by the end of the war, professionalism was on the rise. During the last stage of the Red Stockings as an amateur team, future judge Rufus King played centerfield.

The 1869 Cincinnati Red Stockings, baseball's first all-professional team, were spurred by the leadership of former cricket players George and Harry Wright. The Red Stockings brought in the best players from the East and Midwest. In fact, only first baseman Charlie Gould (front row, far right) was a native Cincinnatian. Touring around the country and outclassing its opponents, the team compiled a record of 57–0.

Charlie "Bushel Basket" Gould was one of the first "good field-no hit" professional ballplayers—excellent at first base, but miserable at the plate. Born in Cincinnati in 1847, Gould played for the Red Stockings in its beginning years, and then when the National League was formed in 1876, he became the new Reds' player-manager. However, after finishing the season at 9–56, Gould was demoted to player only and, in 1879, wound up as the head groundskeeper.

Ormond "Twinkles" Stone wasn't much of a ballplayer, but in 1877 he was caught up in the debate on whether a thrown ball really could "curve" on its path to the batter. Or was it just an optical illusion? As the astronomer at the Cincinnati Observatory, Twinkles (a nickname because of his personality) knew a thing or two about the trajectory of spheres and asserted that the rotation of the baseball as it left the pitcher's hand created a compression of the air in front of it and a vacuum behind, thus causing it to dip and swerve.

FOOT-BALL IS SUCH FUN.

By the mid-1880s, football was creating somewhat of a sports craze on the nation's college campuses. The students were wild for it, though faculty and administrators decried the attention devoted to it and its violent aspect (this in an age of no padding or helmets). As these two cartoons from a Cincinnati tabloid illustrate, football—either by practice or injury—took time away from classroom work, and, as the game became more popular, alumni increasingly became involved by paying ringers to enroll just to play, and by pressuring college officials to overlook the fact that players skipped classes.

In the years after baseball became a commercial enterprise, it wasn't long before the image of the umpire was entrenched in American culture as the reviled arbiter. With money on the line—from fans attending the games and players earning a living—the stakes were high and every decision on the field was analyzed, and often derided. In this 1885 Cincinnati cartoon, the umpire is seen in full armor to withstand the onslaught of disgruntled fans. In the background, an undertaker stands with his coffins at the ready.

"To church," cries the pastor, / "And escape dread disaster."

But they heed not the cry, / And to base-ball do fly.

Another point of contention was Sunday baseball. Cincinnati, with its strong German element in the 19th century, viewed Sunday as a day of recreation—and thus, a day to go to the ballpark. Despite the minister's entreaties in this 1885 drawing, the Reds were playing in the upstart American Association, a new major league whose teams enjoyed Sabbath ballgames.

Cincinnati brewer John Hauck bought the American Association Reds in April 1886 from fellow brewer George Herancourt (the AA wasn't called the "Beer and Whiskey League" for nothing), and, with his son Louis, devised a set of "privileges" or concessions. For $2100, a local company purchased the concession to sell beer at the ballpark—but only Hauck's beer could be sold, of course.

At the end of the 1886 season, Hauck sold the Reds to Aaron Stern (who had sold the team to Herancourt in 1884), and Stern installed Gus Schmelz as manager. In this 1888 photo of the team, Schmelz is seated in the second row, third from the left. To his left is Stern, and next to him is Louis Hauck, who served as club treasurer. The brewers still maintained minority interests in the team.

The 1894 season opened with fanfare and a great deal of promise. League Park had a new grandstand, and pioneer playing great Charles Comiskey (above, lower right) was the manager. Hope and promise led to little, however, as the Reds—back in the National League since 1890 and still selling beer and playing on Sundays—finished the year in 10th place in the 12-team circuit.

Outfielder William "Dummy" Hoy first played for the Reds on the 1894 squad, having previously played in Washington, Buffalo, and St. Louis. He was the first deaf-mute in the professional ranks and enjoyed a 14-year career, five in Cincinnati. Hoy lived in Cincinnati after his playing days, attending the 1961 World Series at Crosley Field. He died on December 15th of that year at the age of 99.

Cincinnati Gymnasium
—AND—
ATHLETIC CLUB,
CINCINNATI, O.

Exercising Hall and Assembly Rooms—
Grand Opera House Building, Vine and Longworth Sts.
Athletic Grounds and Boat House—
Eastern Avenue and Ridgley Street, East End.

Expanding leisure time coupled with community reaction against the "low class" sports led to the creation of athletic clubs such as the Friars Club, the Fenwick Club, and the West End Athletic Club. Many of these groups emphasized physical improvement along with social contacts. In the case of the American German Turners movement, which had its birth in Cincinnati in 1848, there was a distinct effort to make responsible citizens through libraries, social activism, and physical health. The Cincinnati Gymnasium and Athletic Club, shown in this advertisement, was founded in 1853 and, over its first several decades, expanded to include gymnastics, swimming, boxing, and weightlifting.

Dog fighting was a sport refined in the saloon subculture, and it existed for the sole purpose of betting. Hotly debated almost two centuries after becoming a staple activity in tavern back rooms and urban alleys, dog fighting still raises issues of morality and law in sporting life; and it is still a concern in Cincinnati, Hamilton County, and southwest Ohio. The first of these 19th century drawings shows dogs being set at each other, and the second shows Paddy, one of the most famous fighting dogs in the country in the 1880s. Owned by Cincinnatian Dan Kane, Paddy was the feature of a favorable newspaper article in 1884 that extolled his skill in the fighting pit. The article listed the dogs Paddy had beaten in Cincinnati saloons and the fact that he was often backed by bets of $300 to $1000.

Club House, Chester Park, Cincinnati, O.

Boxing was another sport fraught with ethical debate, and one that went in and out of favor with legal authorities. Depending on which way the wind was blowing in Cincinnati, boxers and their followers moved secretly from place to place around the city, and sometimes across the river to Kentucky, in order to stage a match just beyond the reach of the long arm of the law. Completely in the open was the bout between John L. Sullivan, the "Boston Strong Boy," and Dominick McCaffrey on August 29, 1885. The first championship fight to be held in Cincinnati, the match was at Chester Park, a popular resort with swimming, rides, and amusements. A large crowd met Sullivan at the train station and accompanied him to the Chester Park clubhouse. Fighting a seven-round fight with gloves under Queensbury Rules, Sullivan was given the decision, though the referee took several days to render it.

Numerous bicycle clubs were formed in Cincinnati in the 1880s and 1890s, including the Brighton Bicycle Club, shown here. In addition to racing tours around town, there were also indoor races in gyms and athletic clubs. In one instance, a notable race was held by the Cincinnati Bicycle Club in Power Hall in November 1883, on a night that was so frigid that the hall could not be heated, and both spectators and racers shivered throughout the competition.

Some form of bowling has been played in America since 1650, when the Dutch of New Amsterdam first knocked down pins. By 1850, bowling was popular in major cities, and in Cincinnati the game spread rapidly through German American recreation, illustrated by this 1885 cartoon of the alley at the Highland House resort. By 1905, there would be 35 bowling clubs in Cincinnati, including the Kegel Klub Frosch (Frogs), whose large *papier mache* frog became the team mascot.

The German American contribution to the development of sport in 19th century Cincinnati encompassed every aspect, from professional and amateur to "high" and "low" form. The growth of the Turnverein led to halls throughout the city. This drawing is of the West Cincinnati Turners' Hall in the 1880s.

The first sporting organizations formed in Cincinnati were shooting clubs. The Cincinnati Shooting Club #1 was formed in 1831 and the Cincinnati Independent Shooting Club was created in 1834, both clubs given to sportsmanship in game hunting. Competitive target and trapshooting was a sport especially enjoyed by German Americans; this view is the *Schuetzenverein*, or shooting club, on Fairmount Avenue in Price Hill. The tradition continues today with the shooting festivals held by the Catholic Kolping Society.

In 1893, W. Durant Berry was hired by the University of Cincinnati to head its "physical culture" activities. Schooled under James Naismith at the Springfield, Massachusetts YMCA Training School, where he graduated in 1891, Berry introduced basketball to UC, organizing the first games in 1896. Two informal student teams scrimmaged—the Dew Drops and the Pig Toes—and Berry demonstrated fencing at halftime.

By the time this photo was taken of the 1898 UC team, five-man squads were the norm, and the standard uniform included padded football-like pants. It was a rough-and-tumble game. The Cincinnati area had some powerful teams as early as 1894, including the Cincinnati YMCA and the Covington YMCA.

Was Catherine Beecher the first "jazzercise" teacher? Sister of Harriet Beecher Stowe, she was an early advocate of education and physical fitness for women. As part of domestic health and social reform, she believed that women needed regular exercise. In 1856, Beecher wrote her manual on the topic, *Physiology and Calisthenics*, and as part of the curriculum at the school she founded, calisthenics were set to music.

Women's basketball grew as quickly as men's did after the invention of the game in 1891. Though grim-looking, the 1898 University of Cincinnati women's team shown here had much to be happy about: in that year, English instructor Edith Peck donated a basketball to the team so the men's ball no longer had to be borrowed. They were dubbed the "Bloomer Brigade" by the students, and for propriety's sake, their games were played away from the view of men's eyes.

Two

THE COMPETITIVE RUSH
AND THE CHEERS OF FANS

1901–1919

The 1901 Xavier University football team won the Cincinnati Enquirer's Championship of the Interscholastic Football League. However, the other league members—local high schools—protested because XU used college men. The following year the league disbanded, and Xavier scheduled college opponents. Xavier had its moments of football glory, especially in 1950 when they defeated Arizona State in the Salad Bowl. With increasing deficits, however, Xavier dropped its football program in 1973.

Many of Cincinnati's beer halls and evening resorts included sports as part of the entertainment available. The hilltop establishments such as the Highland House included bowling alleys, billiards rooms, and boxing. The bars in the basin were a little less refined. Shown here in its Over-the-Rhine location above Sixth Street, the Atlantic Garden at the turn of the 20th century offered boxing and wrestling matches in what became an increasingly seedy setting that catered to gamblers, showgirls, boxers, and jockeys.

The "Cincinnati Strongman," German-born Henry Holtgrewe was a beloved character in the early 1900s. A gentle saloonkeeper by trade, Holtgrewe was internationally known for his incredible feats of strength, one of which occurred in 1904 at the Palace of the Fans ballpark. Holtgrewe did a back lift of a platform holding the entire Reds team and their opponents, a total weight of 4,103 pounds! (Courtesy German Heritage Museum.)

Scion of the yeast and gin family, Julius Fleischmann was a Republican stalwart in Cincinnati allied with Boss George B. Cox and, at one time, serving as mayor. In 1902, Fleischmann, along with his brother Max, Garry Herrmann, Cox, and a number of minor investors, bought the Cincinnati Reds from absentee owner John Brush. Politicians and baseball were a natural fit, building a fan base and a voting constituency at the same time.

Max Fleischmann ostensibly was the man in charge of the Reds. As president of the club, Garry Herrmann reported the business affairs to Max and made sure the latter approved trades and expenditures. Fleischmann's real interests were elsewhere, however, and involved everything from yachting to big game hunting. More amenable to a playboy life, Fleischmann relished the role of "sportsman." In 1909, he wrote a memoir of his travels—*After Big Game in Arctic and Tropic*.

A natural for the caricaturist, August "Garry" Herrmann was the political right hand of George Cox, running the affairs at City Hall. His political connections had previously earned him positions on the Board of Education and the Waterworks board. Herrmann had a vibrant personality and an appetite for food and drink to match. His florid looks, loud clothes, and diamond jewelry belied the efficient, forceful businessman behind the desk. Herrmann was named president of the Reds, and his national reputation was such that when the National Commission was formed to run the Major Leagues, he was chosen to be chairman, in effect the first *de facto* commissioner of baseball. Herrmann mediated the creation of the modern World Series, served as president of the American Bowling Congress, and was a beloved figure in sporting circles. Even a racehorse was named after him. The four-legged Garry Herrmann won the Champagne Stakes at Belmont in 1900.

The Palace of the Fans sat like a white
jewel in the red brick of the West End.
Owner John Brush built a new grandstand
and façade for the old League Park. The
Palace opened on April 17, 1902, and was
dedicated on May 16. Modeled in part after
the architecture of the Chicago World's
Fair of 1892, the Palace featured scalloped
box seats for the elite and bleachers and
"Rooter's Row" for the everyday fan.
Rooters Row was fronted by chicken wire,
which was installed to protect the players
from the bottles and abuse of the fans, and
to protect the fans from the subsequent
reactions of the ballplayers. What the
architecture signified was that ballparks
had become a major part of a city's physical
identity and that they had a definite role in
municipal boosterism.

In 1908, intrigued by the notion of baseball under the lights, Herrmann listened closely to a pitch by George Cahill, a floodlight manufacturer, to equip the Palace of the Fans for night games. Five light towers were to be placed around the ballpark, each containing 14 arc lights. Three of the towers were erected that August, when Herrmann formed the Night Baseball Development Company and raised $50,000 for the cost; however, an exhibition game to test the illumination was canceled for that year. But by June 18, 1909, Herrmann thought things were ready. His original plan was to match the Reds against an amateur team but, as the day arrived, Herrmann had second thoughts. Having already made a sizeable investment in cash, he was reluctant to invest in personnel, afraid the experiment could result in injury to his players.

That afternoon as the Reds beat the Phillies 4–1, Herrmann did some scrambling and came up with two squads from local Elks lodges, not facing much of a problem in doing so as he was the Grand Exalted Ruler. Before several thousand fans, a Cincinnati Elks team defeated a Newport team from across the river, 8–5. The infield was illuminated nicely, but the outfield was covered in shadows. There were 18 errors in the game. Somewhat satisfied, afterward Herrmann concluded that improvements were needed before another effort could be made. A quarter-century later, in 1935, the Reds would host the first Major League night game.

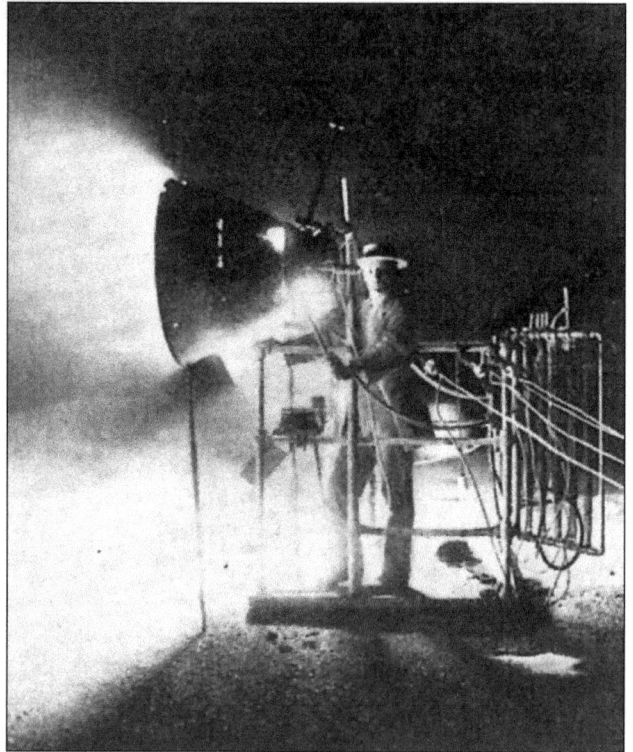

Ballparks have always been more than the scene of athletic endeavors, and have often served as public venues for other events. In this view of the Palace of the Fans in 1910, the Cincinnati Police Department holds a parade and review. Given the number of policemen evident in the photo, one wonders who was left patrolling the streets. Garry Herrmann, always looking for a way to make the team profitable, frequently leased the ballpark for boxing matches, dances, concerts, traveling stage shows, and later, motion pictures. In one case, at least, exception was taken to "extracurricular" activities: Herrmann received a letter in 1921 from the Juvenile Protection League, taking the Reds to task for not monitoring the dances at Redland Field. Too often, the letter stated, vulgar dancing was occurring in the unlighted portions of the grandstand.

During his playing days, Miller Huggins was called "Little Mr. Everywhere." Standing just five feet and six inches, Huggins graduated from Walnut Hills High School and attended UC's College of Law, graduating in 1902. He was a standout second baseman on the semi-pro Cincinnati Shamrocks and, as a minor league player with Saint Paul, he negotiated his own sale to Herrmann and the hometown team in 1904. After his playing career, Huggins managed Babe Ruth and the great Yankee teams of the 1920s, and was elected to the Hall of Fame in 1964.

Born in 1879, Cincinnatian Charlie Grant, an early star in African-American baseball, played from 1896–1916. In 1901, John McGraw, who was managing the American League's Baltimore Orioles, tried to circumvent the racism of the Major League color barrier by signing the light-skinned second baseman as an Indian named Chief Tokahoma. The ruse failed, but Grant continued his great career on African-American teams, including the Cincinnati Stars from 1914–1916.

31

In 1911, it was already recognized that the Palace of the Fans was too small to accommodate the large number of fans following the Reds, and there were not enough box seats to bring in the high-end revenue. So that August, the Reds began demolishing the grandstand. After the season was over, the demolition was completed and work began on a new structure. Redland Field was designed by Cincinnati architect Harry Hake, who commissioned the aerial photograph seen here of Opening Day, April 6, 1912. Redland Field, named by Herrmann after a familiar nickname fans had for League Park, was part of the great ballpark building boom when in a space of seven years, from 1909 to 1915, eleven steel-and-concrete stadiums were constructed in the Major Leagues.

Cincinnatians first began to play golf in 1893, when a course was laid out along Grandin Road on Edmund Harrison's property. Harrison was joined in his new enthusiasm by Nicholas Longworth and Charles Hinkle, and the next year Longworth built a course in one of his pastures. In 1895, the Cincinnati Golf Club was formed with William Howard Taft as president, and the game continued to gain popularity. These postcard views are of the Elberon Country Club on Cincinnati's West Side and the Cincinnati Country Club on Grandin Road in Hyde Park, the home of that first golf organization.

COUNTRY CLUB GRANDIN ROAD CINCINNATI, O.

William H. Taft was the first president to avidly take up golf. Born in Cincinnati in 1857, Taft grew up swimming in the Miami Erie Canal and playing baseball. After attending college at Yale, he returned home to Cincinnati to attend law school and begin his legal career. When he became president in 1909, Taft continued his favorite athletic activities of golf and horseback riding, and his interest in golf caused a boom in the sport. But he was often criticized for devoting more of his time to the links than to the Oval Office. There was a good reason: Taft was a very unhappy president and took refuge in his golf game (he tended to be a poor putter and often yelled at his ball).

I'm going to make a record this trip.

The photo above shows Taft on the course, and the postcard at right mocks him as "Billy Possum," the counterpart to Theodore Roosevelt's teddy bear. With the crest of Yale University in the corner, the card implied that golf was a Republican game of the rich and privileged.

In the early part of the 20th century, Cincinnati boasted a number of exceptional semi-pro teams, such as the Cincinnati Shamrocks, the Mohawk Browns, the Spinney Specials, and the Walnut Hills Superbas. One of the Superbas players, catcher Red Dooin, eventually went on to a 15-year Major League career. This 1909 photo of the Superbas traveling club shows a team that went 27–3 for the season.

Ball diamonds were scattered around the city, usually on the outskirts wherever flat land was available, since the basin had long since been given over to development. This photo is of the fields near what is now Gilbert Avenue on the east side of downtown. The Baldwin Piano factory can be seen at the left, with its stacks of lumber ready to be made into music, and Mt. Adams is in the center background.

Part of the urban Progressive Era efforts to clean up the cities, rid governments of corruption, and make life better for the poor was the Organized Play Movement. As it spread throughout the country, local charitable organizations and citizens' committees took charge of building playgrounds, gyms, and recreation centers for the city's children, trying to provide a healthful environment amid squalor and immoral influences. The notable factor is that many of these facilities were built without local government interference and control. These photographs are of Cincinnati playgrounds circa 1910, showing a Cincinnati Women's Club-sponsored swimming pool on Pearl Street and swing sets in Woodward Park.

The establishment of "settlement houses" was a Progressive Era idea of the late 1800s and early 1900s, setting up institutions in urban areas to help assimilate immigrants into American culture. In addition to immigrants, the urban poor were also assisted. Classes were given in such areas as health and hygiene, job training, childcare, the English language, and—sports. Learning baseball or basketball or boxing not only helped keep young people away from harmful influences like gangs, saloons, and pool halls, but also identified them as "American." This early 1900s photo is of the ball team at a Cincinnati settlement house, the Santa Maria Institute.

Founded and subsidized by donations from philanthropic and religious organizations, settlement houses were often differentiated by religious and ethnic identification. Early urban religious schools also provided instruction in English, vocational and academic training, and sports, along with the teaching of religious heritage and language. In this photograph, young Jewish boys shoot hoops at a playground next to their Talmud Torah school in the West End.

In 1891, the Cincinnati YMCA erected the building shown here, the first fully-equipped Y in the city. In the 19th century, the YMCA organization embraced the concept of "Muscular Christianity"—blending mind, body, and spirit—and this new building provided the equipment for gymnastics and other sports. The Y derived much of its physical training program from the philosophy of the German-American *turnverein*. By World War I, programs were expanded beyond gymnastics to include teams in baseball, football, basketball, and swimming (the champions seen below).

Armory, Cincinnati

The armory on Freeman Avenue served a much larger purpose than training the National Guard to do calisthenics and march in place. As it was with armories across the country, the ONG armory also served as a sort of public sports palace. Gymnastic and track meets, athletic carnivals, bicycle races, boxing bouts, and basketball games were also held there. In 1908, the redoubtable Garry Herrmann staged Cincinnati's first American Bowling Congress Tournament. Sixteen alleys were set up in the armory, and an around-the-clock beer-and-music hall was held in the basement with concert bands entertaining the bowlers and their families.

EXCITING!   **NEW!**   **INTERESTING!**

BASKET BALL
(DOUBLE HEADER)

YALE vs. U. of C.

At O. N. G. Armory, Tuesday, January 3rd,. 8:00 P. M.

1905

To be followed by a Game between the Old Rivals

Christ Church and Y. M. C. A.

Reserved Seats on sale at HENRY STRAUS' CIGAR STORE, S. W. cor. 5th & Walnut.

Of the local basketball teams, the University of Cincinnati was one of several that played some games in the armory. This 1905 ad promoted a game between Yale and UC, which the Yalies won 31–17.

Equally outstanding at hoops as they were at gymnastics and swimming, the Cincinnati Turners basketball team played in competitive leagues against Cincinnati fraternal and religious organizations, holding their own year after year. This photo shows the 1905 team, dressed in jerseys and what were often called "Turner pants" in the sports world, a uniform adapted from the gymnastic togs.

The Cincinnati Turner chapters hosted a major event in the city in 1909, the North American Sports Festival for Turner Organizations. For one week, from June 23 to June 27, German Americans from around the nation thronged the city to compete in traditional activities of the movement. And, because the Turners were all-encompassing in their embrace of "culture"—physical, civic, and intellectual—musical programs were presented with singing societies entertaining the visitors. Demonstrations of calisthenics were given, and the Carthage Fairgrounds became the site for both food and German culture booths and the sports events.

NORDAMERIKANISCHER
TURNERBUND
30. BUNDESTURNFEST
CINCINNATI·O·23-27. JUNI. 1909.

TURNFEST SOUVENIR CINCINNATI 1909

The Reds' ballparks were always noted for the excellence in design and maintenance, the work of groundskeeper Matty Schwab. Schwab was an all-star in his own right, developing new drainage systems, bases, and scoreboards for baseball fields, and sharing them with other groundskeepers. Shown walking the bleachers of Redland Field with another groundskeeper, Schwab paid close detail to his sports garden because that is what the ballfield meant to him. Matty would finesse the slope of the pitcher's mound and the base paths, playing to the strength of each Reds team in each season. A slow infield would benefit fast runners, and the slight grading of the dirt on the foul lines would mean a bunt single or a strike. His meticulous rendering of the field is shown here in blueprint. Schwab worked for the Reds from 1894 to 1963.

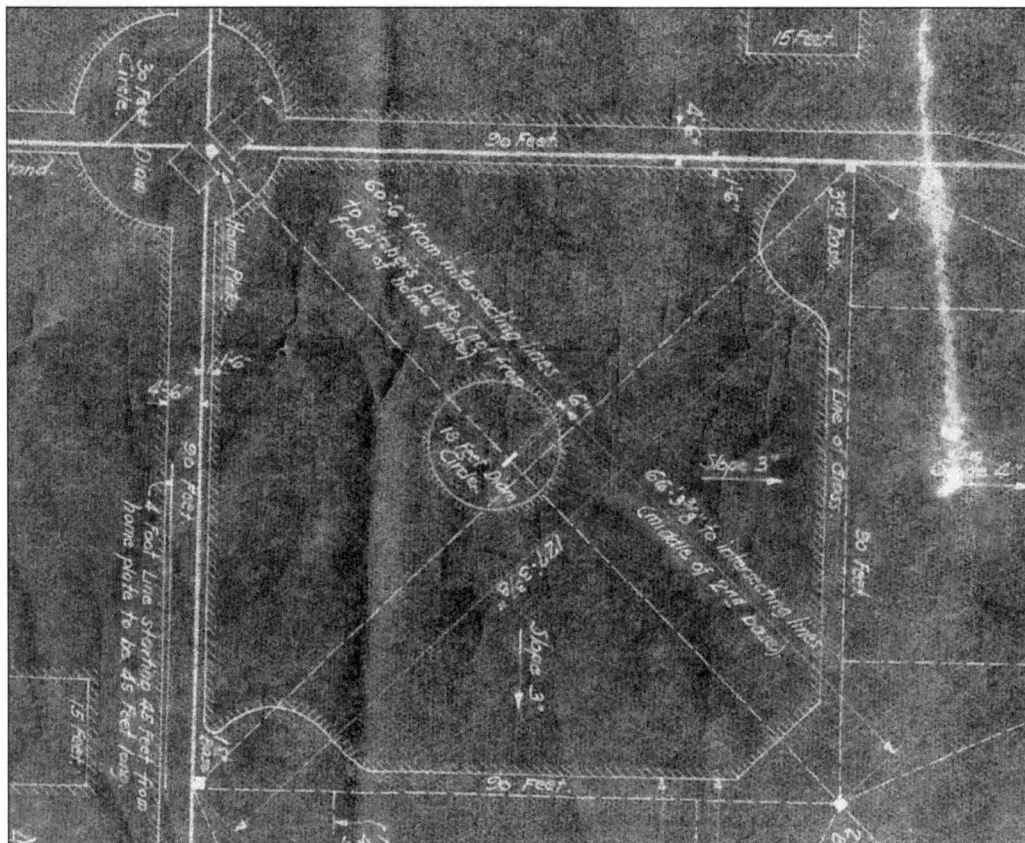

Barnstorming American ballplayers began spreading the baseball creed around the world in the 1880s, and in Japan the sport quickly caught on. Japanese college teams began their own tours to the United States in the early 1900s, and the players were quite skilled at the game. In 1911, the Keio University team, shown here in Japan, embarked on an American tour to play against other university teams, and Cincinnati was on their itinerary. On May 19, Keio played UC at the Palace of the Fans, winning the game 5–3. The next day, they again bested the local college team in eleven innings, 6–4, as Sugase, the Keio pitcher, fanned nine and walked only one. In addition to the victories, the Japanese team also took away with them the innovative design for the infield-dragging equipment devised by Matty Schwab. The next year, UC played a team of Chinese barnstormers, winning 5–3 and, in 1924, welcomed a team from Japan's Meiji University at Redland Field, winning 7–6.

Known as "Eight Stride," Ralph Belsinger (top row, fifth from left) was the first African-American athlete at the University of Cincinnati. Belsinger ran track for UC from 1911 to 1915, anchoring the relay teams and running the mile. After graduating with a degree in education, Belsinger taught in Cincinnati's public school system for four decades.

A bloodsport for the college crowd, "Flag Rush" was an American campus tradition from the 1870s until World War I. One class would hoist a flag to the top of a pole, lock arms around it, and challenge another class to capture it. Captains were chosen, strategies were developed, and the donnybrook could continue for hours. The resulting effects were frequently broken noses and concussions. After years of complaint from parents and college officials, the sport was abolished. This view is of a UC flag rush in 1910.

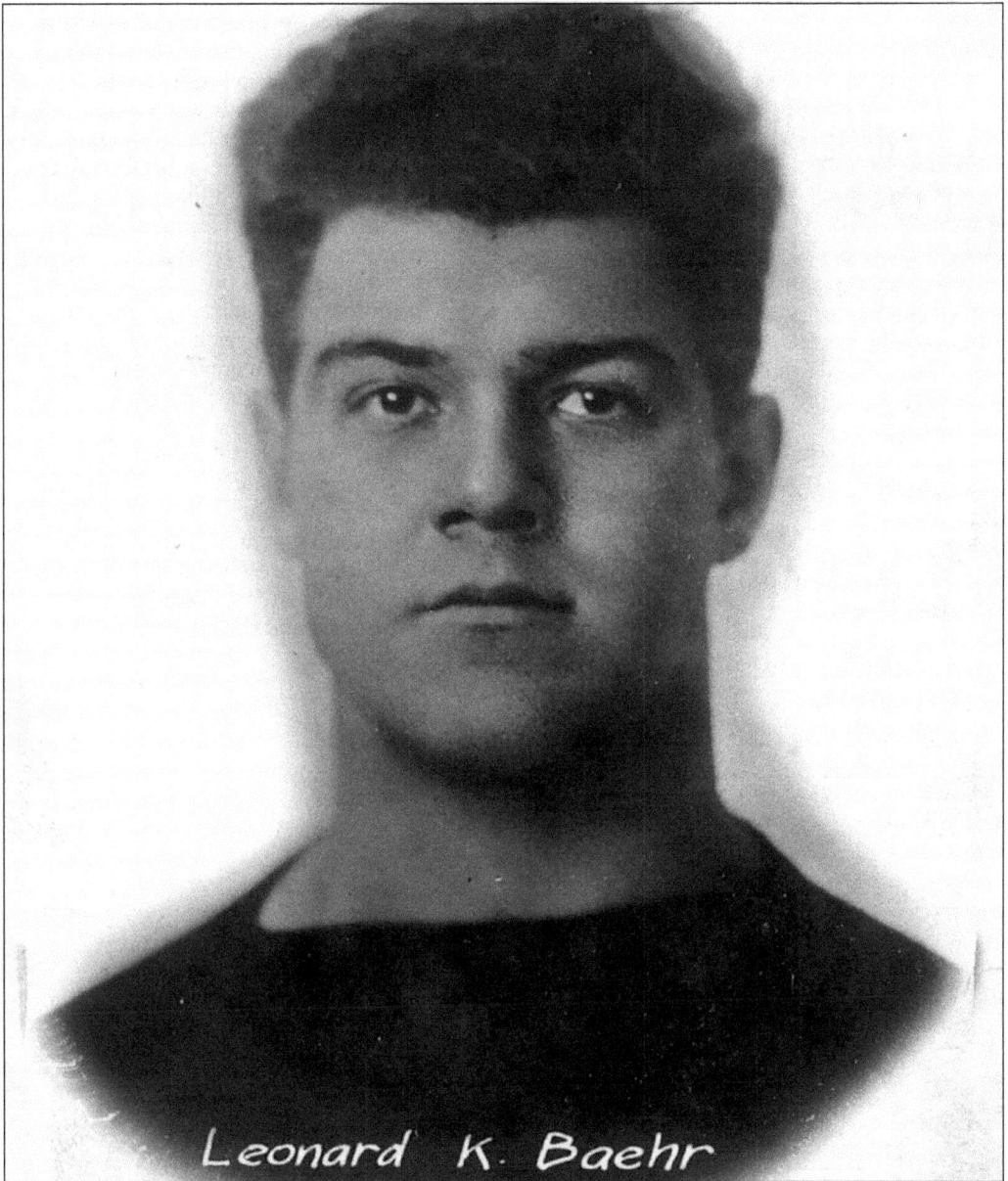

Leonard K. Baehr

Leonard K. "Teddy" Baehr may have been one of the inspirations for the creation of the Bearcat mascot for the University of Cincinnati. An outstanding lineman and back for the UC team, Baehr captained the squad in 1914 and was on the field in a game against Kentucky when a cheer went up—"Come on, Baehr-Cat"—in response to the Kentucky Wildcats. The next year, Baehr earned some spending money by playing football for the semi-pro Cincinnati Celts at Redland Field, along with other former local collegians. With the North Cincinnati Colts and the Avondale Athletic Club, the Celts were just one of a number of strong teams in the Midwest that would eventually give birth to the National Football League. In 1921, the Celts briefly played in the American Professional Football Association, but in 1922 they were closed out of the fledgling NFL. In the 1930s, Cincinnati would have the Redlegs, the Bengals, and the Blades vying for professional status.

UNION PRINTERS' NATIONAL
BASEBALL LEAGUE
TOURNAMENT.

THE MOST UNIQUE CONTESTS IN THE HISTORY OF BASEBALL
ELIMINATION SERIES
FOR THE AMATEUR CHAMPIONSHIP OF THE WORLD.

CLUBS FROM

New York   Cincinnati   Boston   Chicago
Philadelphia St. Louis   Washington   St. Paul
Pittsburg   Indianapolis   Cleveland   Detroit

CONTESTING FOR THE
GARRY HERRMANN TROPHY

GAMES AT
REDLAND FIELD
BEGINNING
SUNDAY, AUGUST 2, 1914
A DOUBLE-HEADER EVERY DAY.   FIRST GAME AT 1:30 P.M.

ADMISSION, 25c and 50c   Box Seats 75c

BOKELOH PRINT. 19 E. THIRD ST.

Beginning as a "printer's devil" in 1870 at the age of eleven, Garry Herrmann maintained a lifelong loyalty to the Typographers Union. It was as an apprentice printer that he acquired the nickname "Garry" because his foreman thought the boy looked like the Italian statesman, Garibaldi. Herrmann's given name of August would henceforth only be used for formal occasions. His devotion to the printers' union, carrying a union card long after he said farewell to ink and press, placed Herrmann in great esteem in the union. With his sportsman's background and involvement in the Reds and Organized Baseball, the annual printer's tournament was named in his honor. An advertising flyer (union printed) promoted the 1914 tournament at Redland Field. The local team, seen below in a photo complete with batboy, hosted printers' teams from around the country.

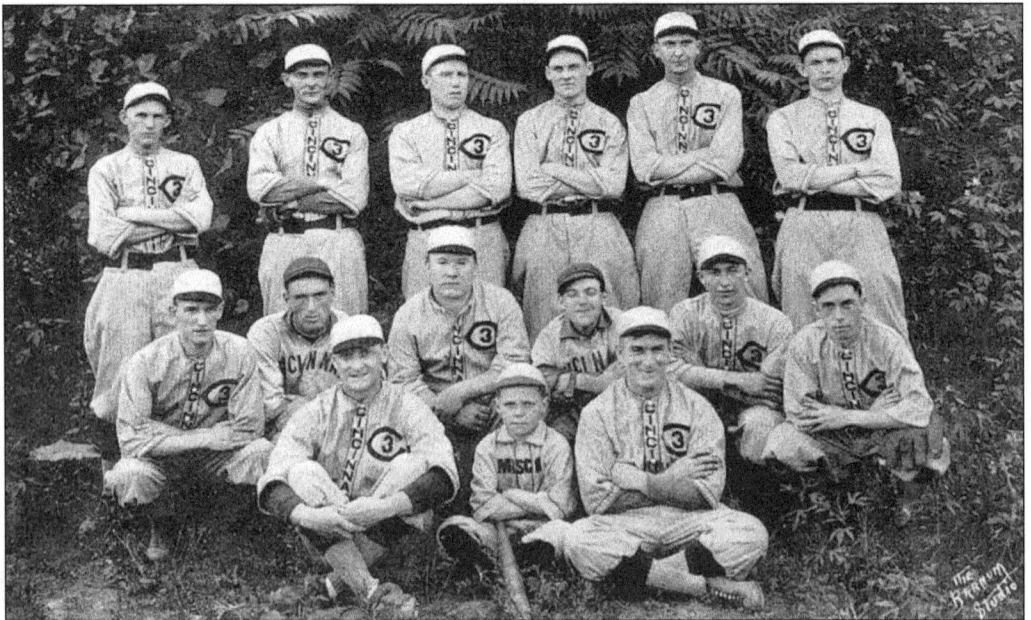

The *Cincinnati Enquirer* called Jim Thorpe the "perfect man" and a "physical paragon" in a 1913 article. Thorpe was just coming off his tremendous achievements at the 1912 Olympics in Stockholm, Sweden, where he won both the decathlon and the pentathlon. Considered the best all-around athlete of his age, Thorpe was already well known for his football days at the Carlisle Indian School. After he was stripped of his Olympic medals and his amateur status when it was discovered he had played a season in the minor leagues, Thorpe turned to the majors and signed with the New York Giants.

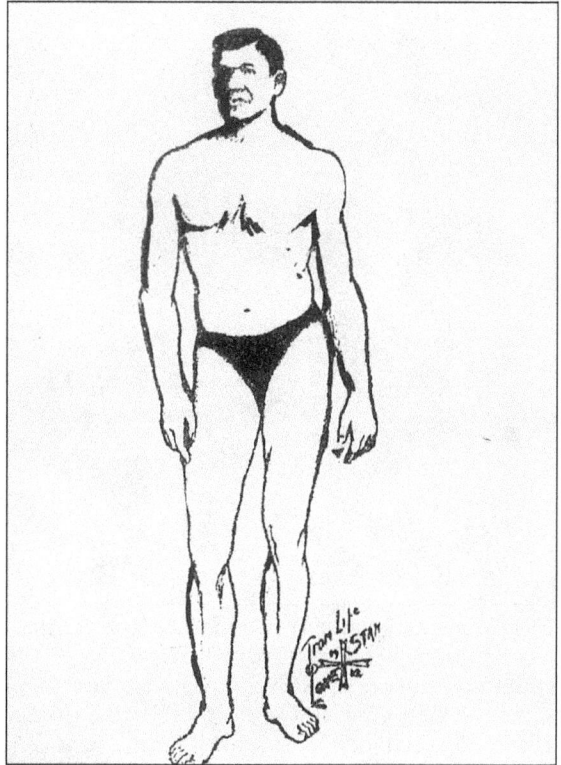

Thorpe's six-year professional baseball career included a stint in 1917 with the Reds, batting just .247 in 77 games. Maybe he couldn't hit the curve ball. Following his retirement from the game in 1919, Jim Thorpe had an outstanding pro football career with the Canton Bulldogs.

47

In 1890, the Cincinnati Gymnasium and Athletic Club decided to broaden the offerings for its members when it created the Cincinnati Gymnasium Boat Club. At the time, boating and swimming clubs on the Ohio River were very popular in Cincinnati. These two early postcards show the Boat Club in the early 1900s and divers who enjoyed it. The boathouse was built in 1892 and lasted for 35 years, until it sank near Coney Island.

Posing for a studio postcard, these Cincinnati swimmers didn't have access to the Cincinnati Gymnasium boat, but the river was still available to them—a number of beaches were located east and west of the city. In addition, indoor pools such as at the YWCA were constructed for women. Women's swimming as a healthy athletic activity was given a boost when Australian champion swimmer and diver, Annette Kellermann, appeared on a tobacco card produced in Ohio in 1907, the same date as this postcard. Kellerman's physical statistics were even listed on the back, and she was one of the first female swimmers to wear a one-piece suit.

The Avondale Athletic Club was founded in 1899 and hosted a Cincinnati Open tennis tournament in its first year. In addition to the clay and brick dust courts, the club also included a swimming pool and golf course. The clubhouse, viewed on the hill above the tennis courts, contained a ballroom and bowling alleys, and the AAC fielded several strong football and baseball teams. In 1911, Xavier University purchased the property to use it for student activities.

Auto racing in Cincinnati caught on very early in the sport's history. Tracks in Oakley and in Sharonville (shown here) were favorite locales for regular races, and road rallies were often created for fans. The Cincinnati Fernbank Dam Association sponsored a rally in 1911 that drew thousands and, in 1916, the Cincinnati Motor Speedway in Sharonville held the first International Sweepstakes Race of 300 miles on Labor Day, attracting 40,000 spectators.

Pictured here is Marjorie Hillas, who coached women's basketball at the University of Cincinnati from 1917 to 1922, compiling a record of 13–3–1. Hillas did have to compromise somewhat to schedule opponents, using women's rules on the road and men's rules (which she favored) at home. Also pictured, from left to right, is the 9–1 team of 1916: (front row) Leona Taylor, Adelaide Saunders, and Julia Hummler; (middle row) Laura McIntyre, Marguerite Tierney, and Sophie Brunhoff; (back row) Olga Rummel and Anita Schreck.

By World War I, the National Commission of Organized Baseball was unraveling. Garry Herrmann, shown here with American League president and fellow commissioner Ban Johnson (at right), was losing control. Gambling infested the game, and Herrmann was increasingly viewed as Johnson's tool when he ruled in favor of the American League over the National League in several player contract disputes, most notably that of future Hall-of-Famer George Sisler. Herrmann decided Sisler should play with the AL St. Louis Browns instead of the NL Pirates.

A former baseball player with the White Stockings and Pirates, evangelist Billy Sunday heard the calling and quit baseball in 1890. Noted for his histrionic preaching with baseball terms and a safe slide into home thrown in, Sunday made his first non-playing appearances in Cincinnati in 1921 before tremendous crowds. The attention might have been because in 1915, he denounced Cincinnati as a "cesspool of rot and filth."

"Prince Hal" Chase was one of the most corrupt players in baseball history. A sterling first baseman and an excellent hitter, Chase had the tendency to make fielding errors at crucial points in the game. He played in the big leagues for 15 years, coming to the Reds in 1916 with a suspicious reputation for gambling on games. After a quiet investigation by manager Christy Mathewson and Garry Herrmann, Chase was suspended in 1918, and although the suspension was overruled, he was banned from Organized Baseball in 1919.

One of the first to raise the red flag on Chase was Reds outfielder Edd Roush. Roush was a cantankerous but brutally honest sort, who brooked no discussion about his own honesty or brilliant play. Though he often had rancorous contract talks with Herrmann, he came through on the field, becoming one of the best centerfielders of his era. Playing for the Reds from 1916 to 1926 and again in 1931, he had a career batting average of .323. Roush was elected to the National Baseball Hall of Fame in 1962.

Hotel Sinton, Cincinnati, Ohio.

The Sinton Hotel was the baseball headquarters in Cincinnati for the opening of the 1919 World Series. That there was gambling on baseball games was no secret at all; it was endemic in the sport. That it had extended to the Fall Classic was an open secret. Gamblers and bookies crowded the Sinton lobby the night before the first game, feeding rumors and looking for the best odds.

Chicago journalist Ring Lardner, one of America's great short story writers, covered the 1919 World Series even though he was about to leave the sports beat. In town for the series, Lardner suspected things were not on the level, and his colleague, Hugh Fullerton, would break the story of the now infamous "Black Sox" scandal a year later. The night before the first game, Lardner gave a hilarious speech to the Reds at Music Hall as they were presented with Rookwood vases, which "will keep them busy all winter wondering what to do with them."

Abe Attell was the bag man for delivering the money to the White Sox players in on the fix—Chick Gandil, Lefty Williams, Ed Cicotte, Swede Risberg, Joe Jackson, Happy Felsch, Fred McMullin, and Bucky Weaver (who was on the level, but knew about it). Attell was a former featherweight boxing champ who began his career in 1900, and after it ended, was well known in betting circles.

ABE ATTELL.

New York gangster Arnold Rothstein was said to be the brains—and the bankroll—behind the conspiracy to throw the series. Rothstein made his money by financially backing operations like bootlegging, horseracing, and illegal gambling. He would escape conviction in the Black Sox scandal and, in the process, become part of American folklore. On November 4, 1929, Rothstein was shot dead following a poker game.

The 1919 World Series was also unusual in that it was scheduled as a nine-game series instead of the usual seven. The Reds took Game 1, 9–1, on October 1. Shown here is that first game and an overflow crowd of more than 30,000 people. The Reds very well might have won the Series whether there was a fix or not; it was a solid team with 96 regular season victories. Be that as it may, the Reds also won Game 2 at Redland Field, dropped the third at Comiskey Park, and then captured Games 4 and 5. The Sox came back to win the next two, but on October 9 at Comiskey, the Reds beat Chicago 10–5 for the team's first world championship. By the following September, the eight White Sox players would be indicted by a Chicago grand jury.

Three

AFTER THE FALL
AND CHANGING TIMES

1920–1939

As women's sports came under scrutiny in the 1920s because of a fear that intercollegiate competitiveness bred unfeminine women, university athletic programs underwent dramatic changes. By the mid-1920s, the University of Cincinnati field hockey team could only play intramural matches on campus.

Still celebrating happy days with the investigation into the World Series gambling scandal months away, the 1920 Reds raise their 1919 championship banner on Opening Day, April 14. Before more than 24,000 fans packed into Redland Field, the Reds beat the Cubs, 7–3.

In another ceremony that same season, Reds manager Pat Moran is presented with an award at home plate before a game with the New York Giants. The Giants wait at the side; manager John "Muggsy" McGraw stands in the middle of the photograph with his back to the camera, arms crossed.

58

Basketball continued its popularity in Cincinnati schools in the 1920s. This view is of the Ohio Mechanics Institute team, playing in their gym at Walnut and Canal. The school began playing basketball in 1914 and continued until 1969, when it became part of the University of Cincinnati. The last OMI team, the Raiders, went undefeated in 1968-69, and won the Junior College Inter-Collegiate League championship.

Up on the hill in Clifton, Hebrew Union College also fielded a basketball team. This photo is of the 1922 squad. Early on in basketball's history in American cities, the game had a number of great Jewish players who embraced the sport in settlement houses and on Young Men's Hebrew Association teams.

This 1921 photo of the Glendale Umbles baseball team was taken at the Wayne Avenue
YMCA in suburban Lockland. Pictured, from left to right: (back row)Wilbur Phillips, Sanford
Wright, Arthur Moore Jr., Leroy Olverson, and Allen Phelps; (middle row) Steve Maxberry,
Alfred Wright, Sam Phelps; ? Olverson, and George Olverson; (front row) Theodore Phelps,
James Dorty, Elmer Harris, and Thomas Hays. (Courtesy of Alfred Wright, Jo Ann Pipes, and
Wyoming [Ohio] Historical Society.)

Another baseball team posing at the Wayne Avenue YMCA was this squad from the northern
suburban neighborhood of Hartwell. Because of the racial segregation at that time, African-
American children from the Hartwell-Lockland-Wyoming-Glendale neighborhoods had to have
their sports and recreational activities at Lockland's Black YMCA. (Courtesy of Jo Ann Pipes.)

As examples of football equipment in the 1920s, one photo shows Mike Palmer of the University of Cincinnati Bearcats building his strength for rushing the ball through the defensive line. Two teammates try to hold him back in a yoke. The other photo shows a faceguard and helmet. Even before football players began using helmets in the late 19th century, there were experiments with face and mouth guards. At first they were leather nose guards on a strap that the player clenched between his teeth. The Goldsmith Sporting Goods Company in Cincinnati devised several types of faceguards, including a metal one covered with foam rubber and tape riveted to the helmet.

Football began at the University of Cincinnati in 1885 and, in 1888, UC played its first intercollegiate game, battling neighboring Miami University to a 0–0 tie. Since then, the games between the two schools have always been intense. At one stage of the rivalry, UC and Miami played their annual game every Thanksgiving Day. This photo is of the 1923 match-up, played in a driving rain on the Clifton campus, where UC defeated Miami, 23–0.

There was a tragic end to that victory, however. Center Jimmy Nippert, one of the most popular students on campus, was kicked in the leg during the contest. Little was thought of his injury. Nippert finished the game, but was hospitalized afterward when blood poisoning set in as a result of the kick. On Christmas day, he died. Nippert's grandfather, Procter & Gamble partner James N. Gamble, contributed $250,000 to UC in order to improve the stadium and provide up-to-date medical facilities.

Adolfo "Dolph" Luque was a great Reds right-hander who was as renowned for his hair-trigger temper as much as he was for his skill on the mound. He was a native of Havana, Cuba, and his antics—carrying a gun, fighting with teammates and opponents—created a media sports stereotype of Latin players as hot-tempered athletes that would persist for decades. In a 20-year career, Luque won 193 games, including a 27–8 record for the Reds in 1923.

Ethan Allen
Baseball Captain 1926

Termed the "dark-haired Apollo" when he was a track, basketball, and baseball star at the University of Cincinnati, Ethan Allen went directly from the campus to the Cincinnati Reds in 1926. Allen once recalled that there was no negotiating of contract terms with Reds president Garry Herrmann—one offer was made and it was take it or leave it. After his playing career, Allen coached at Yale University, where his first baseman was George Bush.

Born in Cincinnati in 1904, DeHart Hubbard was only six years old when he ran in his first track meet. Though beaten badly in the dashes, he persevered and by the time he entered Walnut Hills High School in 1917, was considered one of the best in the city. Hubbard attended the University of Michigan, running the high hurdles and the dashes, and competing in the broad jump. Running in the 1924 Olympic Games in Paris, Hubbard became the first African American to earn a gold medal, winning the broad jump. He graduated with honors from Michigan and came home to Cincinnati to continue his sports career where, in 1926, he organized his own barnstorming basketball team of African-American players, mostly culled from the ranks of the Ninth Street YMCA. Barnstorming was one of the few means at the time for African Americans to participate in professional basketball. The next year he achieved the highest score on a civil service exam for a position with the Recreation Commission, and for the rest of his life, Hubbard trained more Cincinnati athletes, becoming a legend on the playgrounds and tracks.

In the new world of women's sports in the 1920s, eurythmics and interpretive dance were seen as healthy athletic activities. As these pictures show, University of Cincinnati coeds placed their performance props on the football field and then danced up a storm. The serious intent, however, was to show the gracefulness and athleticism of the human form, and to relate it to Greek classical expression.

The photographs shown here are as
artistic as the actions they capture.
In one, Cincinnati coeds perform a
dance movement in classical costume.
Archery was a typical campus sport
for women, as it had been since the
1890s. The photo shows off the strong,
beautiful form of the coed archer.

Pictured here are the Hamilton County high school girls' basketball champions of 1930 from the suburb of Wyoming. Posing, from left to right, are: (front row) Minnie Statzer, Jean Sears, Mary Alice Maham, Jane Graff, Jane Martin, and Berta Gardner; (middle row) Margie Johnston, Marj Warner, Flora Busemeyer, Marj McKee, Julie Schellenback, and Helen Neal; (back row) Don Reams, the manager and Coach Smith. (Courtesy of the Wyoming [Ohio] Historical Society.)

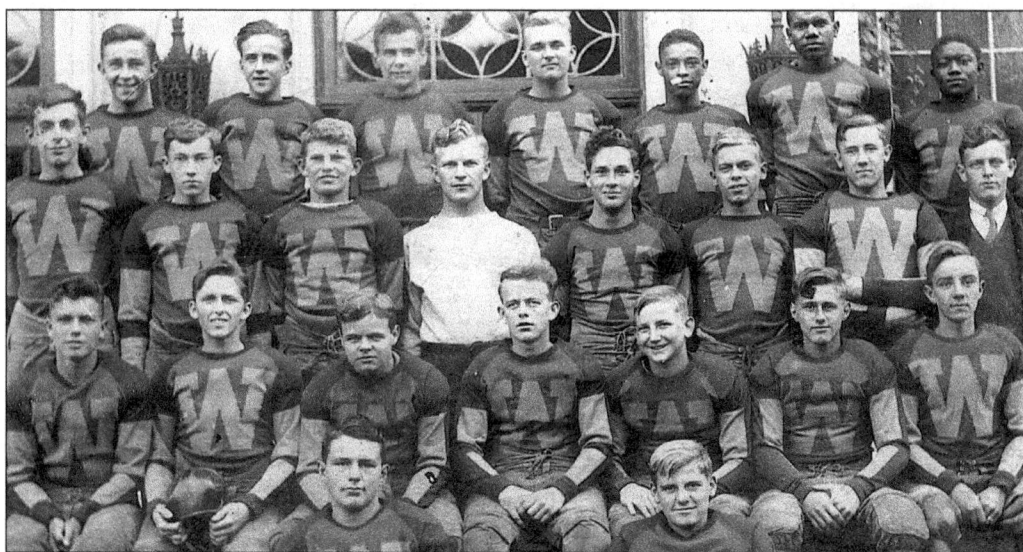

The Wyoming High School football team was also making a name for itself in 1932. Pictured, from left to right, are: (first row) Frank Bonham and Donald Ruscher; (second row) Hugh Mullenix, ? Clark, Bill Butterfield, Robert Maisch, Miles Wachendorf, Carll Shipp, and William Ellis; (third row) Philip Roettiker, Lowe Wiggers, John Bussmeyer, Coach Samuel Selby, Duane Diebel, Bill Sutherland, Richard Stephens, and Carl Maisch; (fourth row) Charles Schwarm, Robert Schwarm, Junior Ruscher, Robert Stevens, John Fox (who won a Congressional Medal of Honor in World War II), and two unidentified players. (Courtesy of the Wyoming [Ohio] Historical Society.)

By 1927, Garry Herrmann's sporting career was coming to an end. Plagued by ill health—heart disease and diabetes, among other ailments—Herrmann gave up the reins to the Reds front office. The previous year, he had applied to the American Professional Football League for a Cincinnati entry, but given the spotty history of local pro teams, the petition was denied. For the last few years of his life, the former political henchman, civic activist, and baseball magnate took it easy, occasionally seeing old friends as they came to visit him. On April 25, 1931, the greatest sportsman in Cincinnati history died at the age of 71, leaving behind a legacy of good cheer and colorful days.

It is unfortunate that Herrmann did not live long enough to see his 1909 experiment with night baseball become a reality. In 1933, the Reds hired the flamboyant Larry MacPhail to be the general manager, and he became one of the most innovative GMs in baseball history. After Powel Crosley Jr. bought the team in 1934, MacPhail advocated another go at night baseball, figuring that with the reduced attendance caused by the Great Depression, such an innovation would attract more fans. Official night games in the Major Leagues debuted on May 24, 1935. President Franklin Roosevelt sent a telegraph signal from the White House and MacPhail switched on the lights. The photographs on this page and the next were taken by Earl Payne, the Cincinnati Gas & Electric engineer who helped design the lights.

The Reds beat the Phillies that night by a score of 2–1, with 20,422 fans in attendance. With Crosley's backing, MacPhail scheduled six more night games for the year, for the seven that had been approved by the National League the previous year. Crosley and MacPhail were right in thinking it would boost attendance: the Reds drew an average of four times more fans for the night games than they did for the day contests.

On the fringes of professional leagues in American basketball have always been barnstorming teams, playing wherever they can, for whatever money they can earn. This photo is of the 1939 Cincinnati Redlegs, a team that lasted for three years. From left to right, the players are Leo Sack; Russell Sweeney; Carl Austing; John "Socko" Wiethe, who became a Cincinnati sports legend; and Clark Ballard, who played and coached at the University of Cincinnati.

FREDDIE MILLER
EX-WORLD'S FEATHERWEIGHT CHAMPION.

Freddie Miller was one of Cincinnati's most engaging boxing champions. Born April 3, 1911, as Frederick Mueller, he won the National Boxing Association featherweight championship in Chicago on January 13, 1933, and then unified the belt under all boxing commissions with a 15-round decision over Nel Tarleton in Liverpool, England, on September 21, 1934. Miller had 237 fights over his career. And, he more than held his own in ballroom dancing and bridge. Cincinnati's first boxing champion, Freddie Miller died in 1962 at the age of 51.

A workhorse pitcher for the Reds from 1933 to 1942, Paul Derringer pitched in 393 games, winning 161. He was a power pitcher, often ranked among the National League leaders in strikeouts. Derringer won key games for the team in their 1939 and 1940 World Series years, including the pennant-winning game in 1939 and the Series clincher in 1940.

Another key pitcher for Cincinnati during the 1930s and 1940s was lefty Johnny Vander Meer. Vander Meer will forever be remembered for a feat no Major League pitcher accomplished before or since: in 1938, his second season with the club, Vander Meer went on the Crosley Field mound against the Boston Braves on June 11 and tossed a no-hitter, 3-0. Four days later at Brooklyn's Ebbets Field, he again fired a no-hitter, beating the Dodgers 6-0.

In the baseball doldrums since the Black Sox scandal of 1919, Reds fans were ready for a winner by the time the team righted itself in 1939. Languishing at or near the bottom of the standings for much of the 1930s, the Reds welcomed the arrival of a tough manager like Bill "Deacon" McKechnie in 1938. He guided Cincinnati to a fourth-place finish in 1938 (up from the cellar the previous year) and, in 1939, he took them to their first pennant in two decades with a record of 97–57. In these photos, Reds fans camp out at Crosley Field to get a chance at World Series tickets against the formidable Yankees and then mob the windows for the prized tickets.

Leading the series three games to none, the Yankees were confident on October 9 in Game 4 that they would go home to New York with the championship. The Reds were ahead 4–2 in the top of the ninth, but let the Yankees tie the game. The top photo shows Joe DiMaggio sliding into third; he would then come home to knot it up. In the 10th frame, Yankee Frank Crosetti walked and was followed by Charlie Keller, who reached first on an error by Red Billy Myers. The next batter, DiMaggio, singled to right, driving in Crosetti. As rightfielder Ival Goodman mishandled the ball, Keller steamed around third to the plate and the second photo shows the result. Keller slammed into Ernie Lombardi, hitting him in the groin and leaving him motionless. DiMaggio, still running, slid across the plate for the 7–4 lead, and for all purposes, the series was over.

In the last photograph taken of him in a Yankees uniform, Lou Gehrig sits with manager Joe McCarthy in Crosley Field's visitor dugout during the 1939 World Series. Gehrig had retired in the spring of 1939, setting the record for consecutive games played at 2,130, since broken by Cal Ripken Jr. in 1995. The Iron Horse was succumbing to the effects of amyotrophic lateral sclerosis (ALS), a disease that would kill him two years later. On July 4, Gehrig was honored in a ceremony at Yankee Stadium, giving his now-memorable "luckiest man on the face of the earth" speech. For games three and four in the World Series, Gehrig traveled to Cincinnati and suited up to watch from the dugout as his beloved Yankees swept the Reds. Even as he approached death, his smile lit up the place, and never in baseball was there a player as gracious and courageous as he. ALS has since become known as "Lou Gehrig's Disease." Gehrig was elected to the Baseball Hall of Fame in 1939; he died two years later, on June 2, 1941.

The sweep complete, a young Dimaggio celebrates with manager McCarthy and catcher Bill Dickey in the locker room at Crosley Field. It was the fourth consecutive world title for the Yankees, as they pounded out 20 runs to the Reds' 8 in the four-game series. DiMaggio batted .313, but the slugging star was rookie outfielder Charlie "King Kong" Keller, who hit .438 and clouted three home runs. The next year, however, would see the Reds once more in the World Series, and the results would be much different.

Four

A COMMUNITY FEELING OF PLACE

1940–1959

Moving toward the completion of its first century, the American Turners movement still maintained a strong influence in German-American communities such as Cincinnati. The emphasis remained on the synergy of physical and mental health, and as this photo of a Cincinnati Turners Club gymnastic demonstration shows, a bit of showmanship as well.

Before the beginning of the first game in the 1940 World Series against the Detroit Tigers, Reds manager Bill McKechnie shakes hands with baseball commissioner Kenesaw Mountain Landis. For the second year in a row, attending the series was a bit of a homecoming for Landis, who grew up in Millville, a few miles north of Cincinnati. The Reds lost that opening game, 7–2, as pitching ace Paul Derringer was knocked out in the second inning.

Taking the hard-fought series in seven games from the Tigers, the Reds joyfully celebrate their title in the clubhouse. Derringer came back from that opening loss to win two games in the series, including a brilliantly pitched 2–1 victory in the final game. Bucky Walters tossed a three-hitter in the second game and also won game six to notch the other two victories.

The revelry continued beyond the ballpark as the team was feted after the series with a ticker tape parade downtown. In this view, fans line Fifth Street to congratulate the champions, the first World Series captured by the Reds since the infamous 1919 win over the Chicago White Sox.

Following the world championship year into the 1940s and 1950s, Crosley Field continued to be a typical example of a neighborhood ballpark. Surrounded by the narrow houses and small businesses of the West End, and framed by the billboards advertising local restaurants and beers, the ballpark was becoming harder to maintain. The Reds also wanted additional seating, but in 1939 voters rejected a bond issue to build a new, larger stadium near the river. It would be three more decades before that plan was realized.

When the Major League ranks were depleted by player enlistments in World War II, Cub president Philip Wrigley gave baseball fans another version of the game in the All-American Girls Professional Baseball League, a circuit lasting from 1943 to 1954. One of the AAGPL players was Cincinnati's Marie "Blackie" Wegman, an excellent fielder who played for Rockford, Fort Wayne, Muskegon, and Grand Rapids in a career that lasted from 1947 to 1950.

Wallace "Bud" Smith became Cincinnati's second native son boxing champion when he won the lightweight division on June 29, 1955, beating Jimmie Carter for the belt. Smith was born in the West End in 1929 and began boxing at the age of twelve, compiling an amateur record of 55–5. He boxed his way to the semifinals of the 1948 Olympics and then turned pro. Smith's career was checkered, however. His matches and managers were controlled off and on by organized crime, and Smith finally retired in 1958. In 1973, he was shot to death while trying to help a woman who was being beaten.

One of the most disgraceful episodes in Cincinnati sports history happened in 1946, when the UC Bearcat football team appeared in the Sun Bowl. After completing an 8–2 season, which included a victory over Big 10 champion Indiana, the Bearcats received a bid to play in El Paso on New Year's Day. However, the invitation made it clear that no African Americans would be allowed to play. That meant leaving star end Willard Stargel behind. Overruling the protests of UC president Raymond Walters, the school accepted the bid anyway and racism won out. Stargel was a prominent athlete at UC, in basketball and track as well as on the gridiron, and a World War II veteran. UC beat Virginia Tech 18–6; Stargel became a long-time coach and teacher in the Cincinnati public schools. In this photo of the 1946 team, he is in the top row, fourth from left.

Two of the top players in tennis history, Tony Trabert(left) and Bill Talbert (right), were from Cincinnati. Talbert, older than Trabert, had been a top player for years and served as a mentor to the junior player. These photos are from the 1951 Cincinnati Open tournament in which Trabert came from behind in a grueling match to win the singles finals, 5–7, 4–6, 6–4, 6–3, and 6–4 over Talbert.

A meeting of two great basketball minds: Socko Wiethe was a sports star at Xavier University and, after playing pro football for the Detroit Lions, coached the University of Cincinnati basketball team from 1946 to 1952, bringing them into the national spotlight; George Smith (at left), Wiethe's assistant and successor, coached the Bearcats from 1952 to 1960, leading Oscar Robertson's squad to the Final Four in 1959 and 1960.

College basketball became big-time in the 1940s and 1950s, propelled into popularity by the Madison Square Garden double-headers, and more attractive to gamblers—with the development of the point spread. One of the schools caught in the scandals of the early 1950s was Long Island University. In this 1950 Garden match-up, the LIU Blackbirds were favored to beat UC by seven. Crooked players saw to it that their team lost to the Bearcats, 83–65.

JERRY PHILIPS

LONG ISLAND U. vs. U. OF CINCINNATI
CITY COLLEGE vs. SYRACUSE UNIV.

MADISON SQUARE GARDEN   FEBRUARY 23, 1950

24c, N. Y. C. SALES TAX 1c   25c

Heavyweight Ezzard "The Cincinnati Cobra" Charles became the third of Cincinnati's boxers to win a world's championship. In 1949, with a solid amateur and Armed Forces career behind him, Charles beat Jersey Joe Walcott for the title. The next year, he beat an aging Joe Louis to retain it, but it was the ring battles that Charles had with Rocky Marciano, especially their bout in 1954, that ensured his place in the minds of boxing fans. In ranking the legendary heavyweights, Charles is accorded as being one of the hardest punchers of all time.

LOUIS and CHARLES

EZZARD CHA...
the
Heavyweight Cha...
of The Worl...

One of the greatest coaches in Cincinnati football history was the incomparable Sid Gillman, who coached the UC Bearcats from 1949 to 1954, compiling a 50–13–1 record. Gillman was an outstanding innovator in the game, originating the use of film to break down position roles, creating option plays, and developing the position of split end. From UC, Gillman went to the NFL in a coaching career that landed him in the Pro Football Hall of Fame.

An outstanding team leader for Gillman was Glenn Sample, an undersized physical specimen with an oversized instinct for the game. Sample played for Gillman from 1950 through 1952, serving as captain his senior year and helping the team to records of 8–4, 10–1, and 8–1–1. Sample later became the baseball coach at UC, retiring in 1992 with 403 victories. Since 1980, he has been the official scorer, with Ron Roth, of the Cincinnati Reds.

On December 18, 1954, the Armory Fieldhouse on the University of Cincinnati campus was officially opened, replacing the ancient Schmidlapp Gymnasium. The Bearcats did it in fine fashion, too, trouncing Indiana University, 97–65. James Allen, a 1919 UC alumnus, designed the structure, and it served the varsity well over the years: 247 wins against 29 losses. The biggest Fieldhouse crowd (8,192) was on February 6, 1960, when Oscar Robertson became the NCAA career scoring leader.

Pittsburgh native Jack Twyman hadn't thought about attending UC until Socko Wiethe invited him for a tryout and had the Bearcat players rough him up. Twyman played just as tough, and Wiethe offered him a scholarship. "Smokey" Twyman became an All-American, putting up 1,598 points from 1953 through 1955.

In the autumn of 1953, Brooklyn schoolboy Sandy Koufax came to the University of Cincinnati on a basketball scholarship and with the purpose of studying architecture. As a starter on the UC freshman squad (top row above, fourth from left), Koufax averaged 9.7 points per game and helped lead the team to a 12–2 record. In the spring, he decided go to out for the baseball team (top row below, fifth from left). In high school, Koufax already had commanded some interest from professional scouts with a blazing fastball. In the 1954 season, Koufax pitched his way to a 3–1 record, striking out 51 batters in 32 innings. In a game against Louisville, he fanned 18 in just eight innings, at the time a school record. The Brooklyn Dodgers saw his potential and signed him after the season. Sandy Koufax became one of the most dominating pitchers in the 1960s and was elected to the Baseball Hall of Fame in 1971.

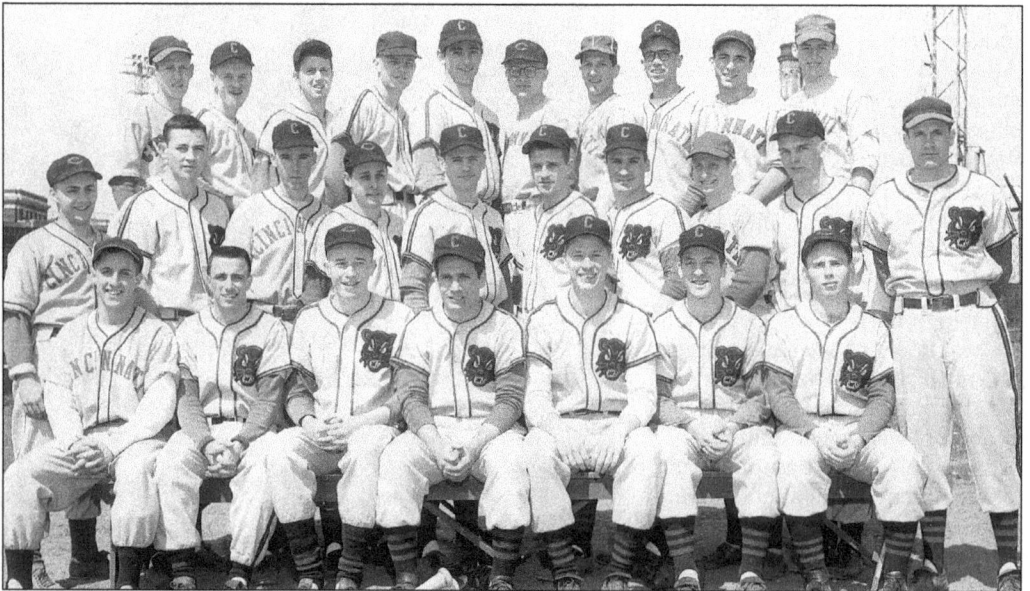

In the 1950s, women's sports started to become stronger on college campuses, though it greatly lagged behind men's athletics. Many of the teams still played intramural games, but there was some movement toward competing against nearby colleges and universities. These two University of Cincinnati photos show that field hockey and fencing continued to be popular sports. Women's athletic programs were part of the College of Education programs and coaches were typically selected from the faculty for physical education, rather than hired strictly for coaching duties.

Women's basketball came into its own in the 1950s and was one of the first sports to look again to intercollegiate play. The Women's Athletic Association, comprised of students and faculty advisors, governed their own activities, apart from the Department of Athletics. These UC coeds played their games in Beecher Hall, originally called the Women's Building, built on the Clifton campus specifically to house women's academic and physical fitness programs. Women's collegiate basketball would not recover from the changes of the 1920s until 1970, when intercollegiate schedules were again fully implemented. In addition to basketball, softball remained a popular physical education class. In a vibrant photograph shown here, the ball is just about to reach the second baseman as the runner approaches the bag.

In 1925, the Coney Island Racetrack opened, offering the first thoroughbred racing in Cincinnati since the Oakley Race Course was converted to auto racing in 1910. Located next to the Ohio River, the Coney Island track immediately became a favorite, attracting the top horses from around the country. After the disastrous flood of 1937, the racetrack was renamed River Downs, as it remains today. In this 1950s-era view, the crowds come out on the opening race day of the season. A counterpart to horse racing in Cincinnati was the heavy betting action from the 1930s to the 1960s. Centered in the neighborhoods of Elmwood Place and Hartwell, saloons and cafes like the Maple Club (run by Cincinnati's "Bookie King" Ike Hyams), the Valley Cigar Store, and the Linden Bar all took bets in back rooms. The establishments tried to legitimize their wagering by stating that they only offered "all sporting results by wire," but law officials moved in and, by the mid-60s, had the bookies on the run.

If ever there were a place in Cincinnati that could be called a mecca for sports, it would be the venerable Cincinnati Gardens, home to basketball, boxing, hockey, wrestling, rodeos, hockey, and soccer. Built in 1949, the Gardens opened the night of February 22 with an exhibition hockey game between the Montreal Canadians and a team that would become the Montreal minor league affiliate, the Cincinnati Mohawks. In addition to the Mohawks from 1949 to 1958, the Gardens was also the hockey home of the Cincinnati Swords from 1972 to 1974, the Cincinnati Cyclones from 1990 to 1997, and the Cincinnati Mighty Ducks from 1997 to the present. By the late 1970s, the Gardens was fading, both in upkeep and events, as the new Riverfront Coliseum provided competition. Purchased by Jerry Robinson in 1981, plans to use it as a warehouse were scrapped, and Robinson transformed it once more into a viable sports arena.

Although the Cincinnati Gardens facility was really constructed for hockey game layouts (modeled after the Maple Leaf Gardens in Toronto) it was always viewed as a multipurpose venue, whether the event was boxing or the Beatles, Elvis or roundball. The concrete reliefs on the exterior of the building—hockey, basketball, and boxing—add architectural luster to a Cincinnati landmark. In basketball, besides the Royals from 1957 to 1972, the Gardens also hosted the Xavier Musketeers and the UC Bearcats, and the Cincinnati Slammers from 1984 to 1987. (Photos courtesy of Joan Fenton.)

Hockey became a favorite sport in Cincinnati after the Gardens opened. The Mohawks were always competitive and, as this 1951 photo shows, gave as good as they got. In a game against Hershey, the Mohawks' Jean Denis and Hershey's Norm Corcoran get into a fight. After the referee separated them, Denis was hit in the head with a stick, leading to an all-out brawl between the two teams.

The Gardens was a wonderful place to enjoy hockey in the 1950s. Every fan seemed to be on top of the game. It was an intimate arena, with the concession smells of Cincinnati beer and brats surrounding the action on the ice. Cincinnati has been a hockey town, off and on, for more than half a century, especially in the last decade as both the Gardens and Riverfront Coliseum (*cum* The Crown *cum* The Firstar Center *cum* The US Bank Center) have hosted hockey. In addition to the Mohawks from 1949 to 1958, there have been the Wings (1963–1964), the Swords (1972–1974), the Stingers (1975–1979), the Cyclones (1990–present), and the Mighty Ducks (1997–present).

CHUCK HARMON *3rd base* **CINCINNATI REDLEGS**

Chuck Harmon was the first African American to play for the Cincinnati Reds, joining the club in April of 1954. Already 28 years old when he appeared with the Reds, Harmon was an outstanding basketball player at the University of Toledo in the 1940s, during their glory years of playing in the National Invitational Tournament. His baseball career was a short one, lasting only four years with three different teams. This photo is of Harmon on a 1955 trading card.

In 1958, the Cincinnati Reds established their own team hall of fame, recognizing the outstanding players for the club over the past decades. For that inaugural class of hall-of-famers, the Reds held a special ceremony at Crosley Field. Pictured, from left to right, are Bucky Walters, Ernie Lombardi, Paul Derringer, Johnny Vander Meer, and Frank McCormick.

95

Little Roy McMillan was a Gold Glove shortstop for the Reds in the 1950s. The Texas native was the first shortstop to win the award when it was instituted in 1957. He was just an average hitter, but one of the outstanding shortstops in baseball, noted for his durability and his dependability on anchoring the Reds up the middle with second baseman Johnny Temple. In this 1959 photo, McMillan is shown as a base runner, colliding with Giants second baseman Daryl Spencer, who covered first base on a pickoff throw from catcher Bob Schmidt. McMillan had broken for second on a bunt attempt by Reds pitcher Orlando Pena.

When Oscar Robertson came to the University of Cincinnati in the autumn of 1956, he was only the fifth African American to play basketball for the school. The much-heralded Indianapolis high school champion soon proved to be the greatest ever to wear the red and black. Three times the "Big O" was the College Player of the Year, and he was known as much for his ferocious rebounding as he was for his accurate passing and smooth jump shot. As the only African-American member of the team at the time, Robertson played through the racism he faced to excel as no college player before him had done.

Maurice Stokes was a rising star in the National Basketball Association in 1955, when he came out of tiny Saint Francis College in Pennsylvania. Playing for the Rochester Royals, Stokes was a powerful, agile forward who could move the ball, rebound, and shoot. By the time the Royals moved to Cincinnati in 1957, many thought Stokes was on the way to the Hall of Fame.

Stokes would be a strong part of the 1957–1958 Royals squad, pictured from left to right: (front row) Dick Duckett, Richie Regan, George King, and coach Bobby Wanzer; (middle row)John Mengelt, Jim Paxson, Clyde Lovellette, and Tom Marshall; (back row) Dick Rickets, Jack Twyman, Stokes, Dave Piontek, and the trainer.

On March 12, 1958, against the Minneapolis Lakers in the last game of the season, Stokes fell hard to the court and hit his head. He left the game, but thought little of the injury. After a playoff game against the Detroit Pistons three days later, the Royals were flying home to Cincinnati when Stokes collapsed and went into convulsions. Rushed to the hospital upon landing, he was diagnosed with post-traumatic encephalopathy. He couldn't walk or speak and his career was over. Teammate Jack Twyman stepped in and became Stokes' legal guardian, raising funds for rehabilitation and care for the next twelve years. Stokes regained some speech and movement due to Twyman's work on his behalf. The courage of Stokes and his friendship with Twyman has become one of the great stories in American sports.

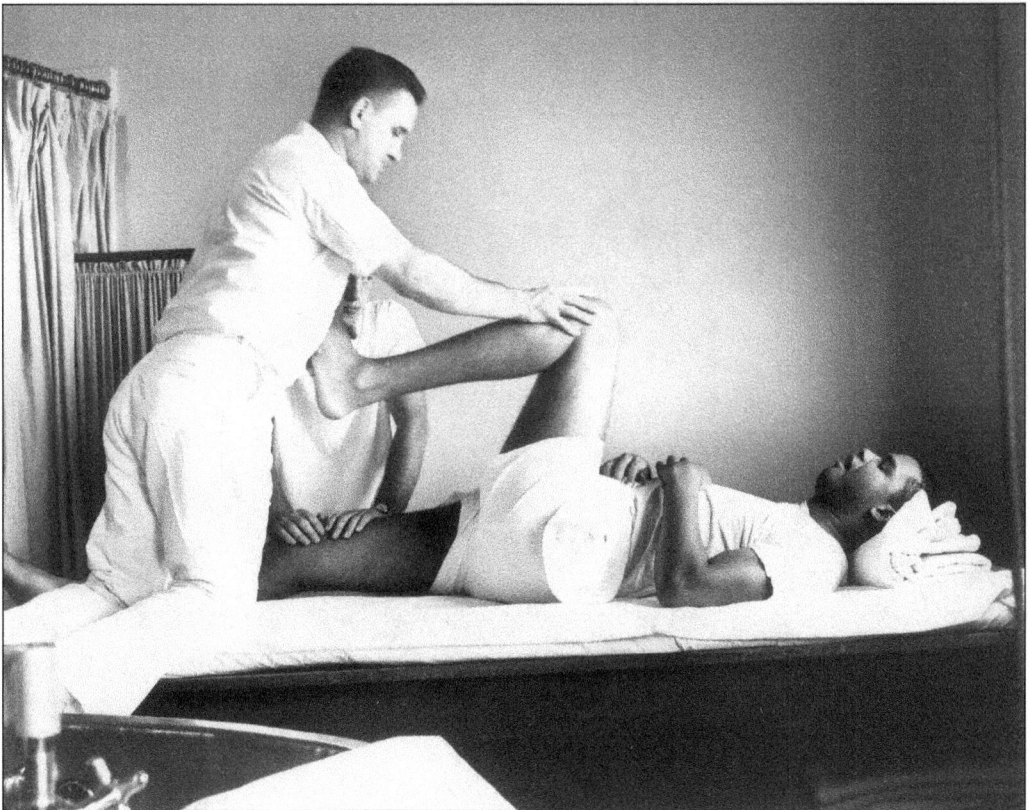

In a visit to the Cincinnati Gardens to see his old team play against the Philadelphia Warriors, Maurice Stokes poses for a photo at courtside with Twyman and Warriors center, Wilt Chamberlain. On April 6, 1970, Maurice Stokes died of a heart attack and was buried on the campus of Saint Francis College.

It looks like quite a mismatch, going up against a trio of great Warriors at once. In this Gardens shot of a Royals-Warriors game, Dave Piontek goes for a lay-up as Chamberlain positions to block his shot. Coming to help Wilt are Paul Arizen, behind Piontek, and Tom Gola moving into the scene.

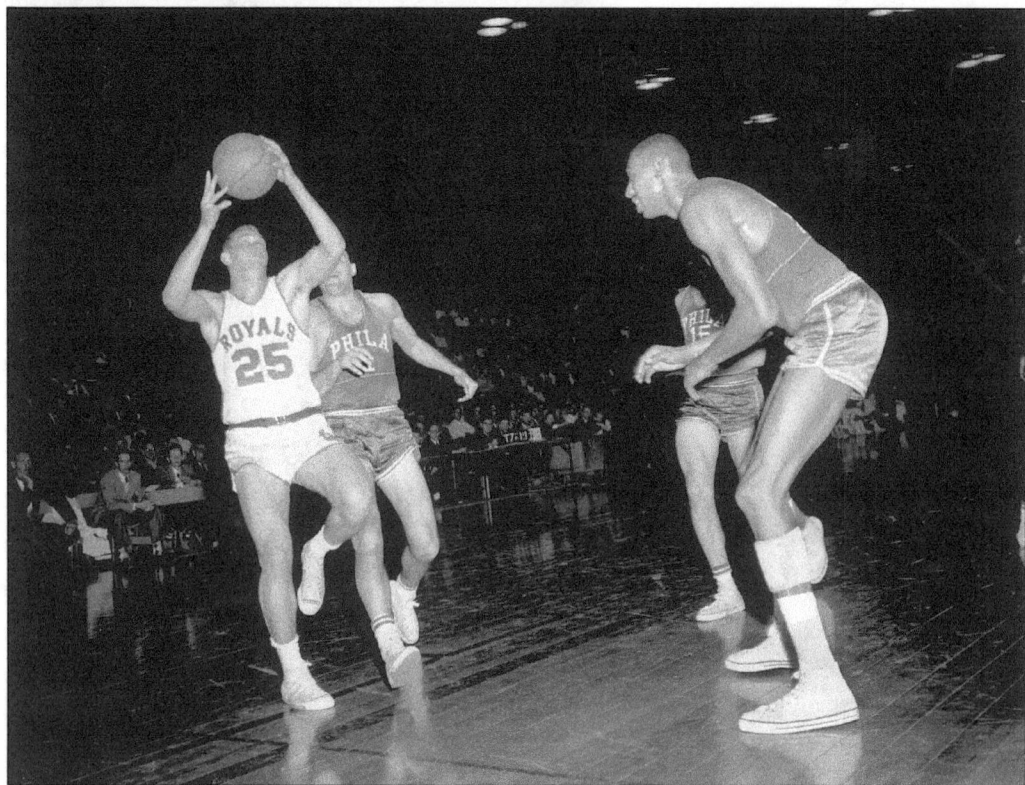

Five

Sport Titans and Urban Rejuvenation

1960–2000

The 1960 Cincinnati Royals, from left to right: (front row) Arlen Bockhorn, Ralph Davis, coach Charlie Wolf, Win Wilfong, and Phil Rollins; (back row) Jack Twyman, Bob Boozer, Hub Reed, Phil Jordan, Wayne Embry, Larry Staverman, and Oscar Robertson.

Having led his hometown Middletown High School team to two state championships, his Ohio State University team to a national crown, and winning an Olympic gold medal, Jerry Lucas joined the Cincinnati Royals in 1963. Shifting to forward, he teamed up with Oscar Robertson and Jack Twyman to make the Royals a championship contender. Lucas was one of the great rebounders in the game and proved his worth not only to Cincinnati, but to the San Francisco Warriors and the New York Knicks in an eleven-year career.

Oscar Robertson was the most complete player of his era in the NBA. Immediately starring for the Royals as a territorial draft choice in the fall of 1960, he became the Rookie of the Year. He was the prototype of the modern big guard, standing 6 feet and 5 inches, and weighing 220 pounds, adding strength to his agility. In the 1961-1962 season, Robertson earned his legendary "triple-double" for the year: 30.8 points per game, 11.4 assists, and 12.5 rebounds. In 1997, he was named one of the top 50 NBA players of all time.

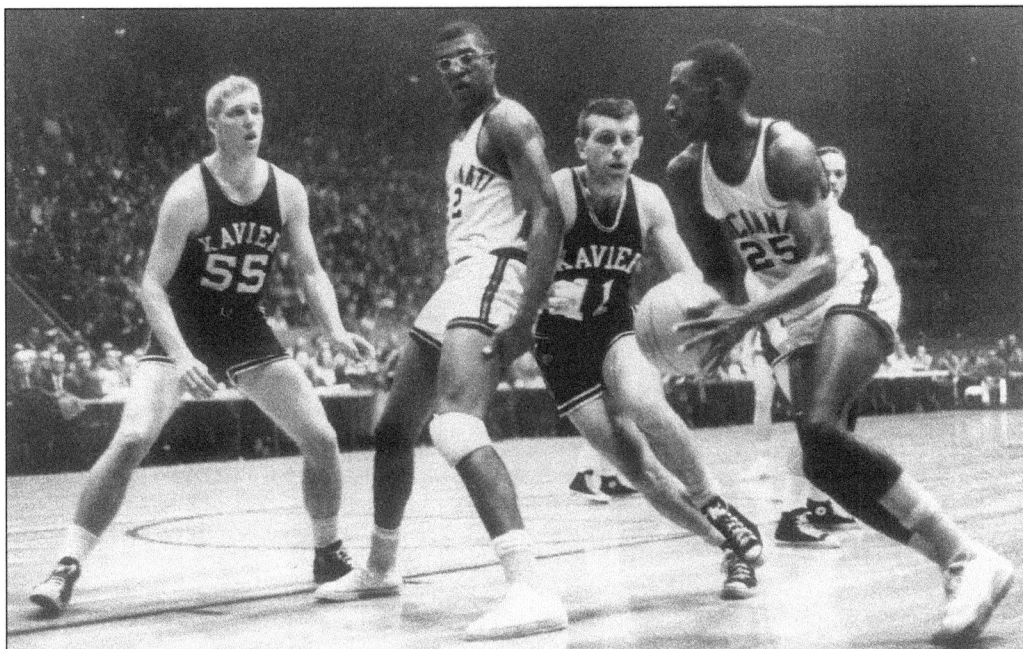

Building a national reputation throughout the 1950s, the University of Bearcats reached the top of the college basketball world in 1961 and 1962, under coach Ed Jucker, when they won back-to-back NCAA championships, beating the Ohio State Buckeyes in the title game each time. In 1963, the Bearcats just missed a third title when they lost to the Loyola of Chicago Ramblers in overtime. In this photo of a game against archrival Xavier University, Paul Hogue sets an oak tree-like pick for Tom Thacker.

River Downs remained a popular feature of Cincinnati sports in the 1960s. This photo shows the horses coming out of the gate to begin the race. In addition to hosting some of the best horses of their times, such as Black Gold, Coax Me Chad, and Spend a Buck, River Downs also marked the debut of one of the greatest jockeys of all time, Steve Cauthen, on May 17, 1976.

103

In 1962, Reds general manager William O. DeWitt organized an investment group to purchase the team from the Powel Crosley Foundation for $4,625,000, the first change in ownership since 1934. The Reds had just come off their unexpected pennant-winning season of 1961, bolstered by trades DeWitt made, and the future looked very bright. DeWitt immediately began lobbying for a new ballpark, something that had been discussed in earnest by the Cincinnati City Council since the late 1950s. DeWitt is shown here at spring training with the Reds in 1961, conferring with manager Fred Hutchinson.

A fireballing right-hander, pitcher Jim Maloney anchored the Reds staff in the early 1960s. During eleven seasons with the Reds, from 1960 through 1970, Maloney pitched three no-hitters, 30 shutouts, and won 134 games.

THE CINCINNATI REDS
1961 — National League

Home of Baseball's First Professional Team—1869

1961 "Lineup" (with Players' Age, Height, Weight) — Left to Right

TOP ROW: (Staff)	RAY EVANS (Equip. Mgr.)	RAY SHORE (A. Bul Prer.)	JIM TURNER (Coach)	FRED HUTCHINSON (Manager)	DICK SISLER (Coach)	REGGIE OTERO (Coach)	OTIS DOUGLAS (Phys. Cond.)	AVERY ROBBINS (Trav. Sec'y.)
3RD ROW: (Pitchers)	JIM O'TOOLE (24, 6-0, 192)	BOB PURKEY (31, 6-2, 194)	JAY HOOK (24, 6-2, 182)	JOEY JAY (25, 6-4, 229)	KEN HUNT (27, 6-4, 220)	JIM BROSNAN (31, 6-4, 216)	SHERMAN JONES (26, 6-3, 219)	BILL HENRY (33, 6-2, 185)	JIM MALONEY (20, 6-2, 190)	HOWIE NUNN (25, 6-0, 176)
2ND ROW: (Inf. & C.)	DON BLASINGAME (29, 5-10, 160)	GENE FREESE (27, 5-11, 185)	ED KASKO (30, 6-0, 180)	GORDY COLEMAN (26, 6-1, 205)	JOHN EDWARDS (C-21, 6-4, 210)	DICK GERNERT (33, 6-3, 210)	JERRY ZIMMERMAN (IC-26, 6-2, 185)	LEO CARDENAS (22, 5-11, 150)	ELIO CHACON (24, 5-8, 143)
1ST ROW: (Outfield)	VADA PINSON (22, 5-11, 176)	WALLY POST (31, 6-1, 215)	GUS BELL (33, 6-1, 190)	PETE WHISENANT (31, 6-2, 198)	FRANK ROBINSON (25, 6-1, 184)	JERRY LYNCH (30, 6-1, 189)			

IN FRONT: BILL FERGUSON (Bat Boy)   NOT SHOWN: DR. RICHARD BOHDE (Trainer)

Litho in USA by Color-Concern Co. for Cincinnati representation. Sohio Mul-Tint Associates.
Color Separations by Tru-Color.

SOHIO   Presented by The Standard Oil Co.

The 1961 Cincinnati Reds exceeded all expectations. Finishing in 6th place in the National League in 1960, the new season held some hope, as Bill DeWitt obtained catcher John Edwards, pitcher Joey Jay, and infielders Don Blasingame, Gordy Coleman, and Gene Freese over the winter. Manager Hutchinson led the team to a 93–61 record, with Frank Robinson clouting 37 homers and 124 RBIs and Jay winning 21 games. In the World Series against the Yankees, the Reds lost in five games.

In the first of 4,236 hits, on April 13, 1963, rookie Pete Rose smacked a triple off Pirate pitcher Bob Friend. The Reds may have lost that particular game, 12–4, and finished a mediocre season in 5th place, but Rose won Rookie of the Year honors.

105

The opening day for the baseball season has always been a major event in Cincinnati, with the Findlay Market Parade and ceremonies at the ballpark. It is the Queen City version of "hope springs eternal." This photo is of opening day on April 13, 1964, as 14 College-Conservatory of Music coeds from UC present bouquets to the players prior to the National Anthem.

Joe Nuxhall first joined the Reds in 1944 at the age of 15; with the rosters short of regular players because of World War II, the Reds gave the teenager a chance. Nuxhall was shelled in his debut, but eight years later he was back, playing for the Reds from 1952 to 1960, and again from 1962 to 1966. Since 1967, the "old lefthander" has been a radio broadcaster for the team. In this 1960s-era view, Nuxhall lunges to tag out a batter who had dragged a bunt down the first base line.

Though he is a Cincinnati baseball legend, Don Zimmer only spent a short time on the hometown team. Zim graduated from Western Hills High School and played on a national champion American Legion team. An all-purpose infielder, Zimmer played 12 seasons in the Major Leagues, including 63 games for the Reds in 1962. Serving more than a half-century in the game, Don Zimmer has managed four teams and coached for several others, including the World Champion Yankees under Joe Torre.

DON ZIMMER
Cincinnati Reds

As the traffic of Interstate 75 roared by Crosley Field in the 1960s, its West End neighborhood was rapidly deteriorating. Parking for the games was hard to come by, even with a few lots put up here and there where homes had been demolished, and the time was ripe to build elsewhere. The 1960s represented another boom in ballpark construction in America's cities, and Cincinnati would join them.

The last game played at Crosley Field was on June 24, 1970, when the Reds beat the San Francisco Giants, 5–4, and baseball ended at Findlay and Western after nine decades. In a post-game ceremony, home plate was removed and flown by helicopter down to the river and the new stadium. By 1971, Crosley was used as an auto impound lot and, in 1972, it was demolished. Crosley Field was no more. Today, there is an industrial park on the site and a marker indicates the location of the legendary ballfield.

Cincinnati mayor Eugene Ruehlmann could be considered the father of Riverfront Stadium. Ruelmann did the necessary political legwork to secure funding and voter approval for the multipurpose stadium to house the teams of new Reds owner, Francis Dale, and Bengals chief, Paul Brown.

The first ballgame in Riverfront was on June 30, 1970, the Reds losing to the Braves 8–2 before 51,000 fans. Henry Aaron hit the first home run in the new park. The fans were happy; the stadium was bright and new, and it built enthusiasm for a decade of some the greatest Reds teams in the city's history.

One of the most memorable plays in baseball history occurred shortly after the Reds moved to their new home. On July 14, Cincinnati hosted the All-Star Game, and named to the National League squad were Tony Perez, Johnny Bench, Pete Rose, Wayne Simpson, and Jim Merritt. In the bottom of the 12th inning, the score knotted 4–4 with two outs, Rose lined a single, moved to second on another NL single and, two batters later, attempted to score as Cub Jim Hickman hit a single to center field. Rose rounded third and barreled for home as the throw from centerfielder Amos Otis came to the plate. Without any hesitation, Rose bowled over catcher Ray Fosse to score the winning run. These two photos show the beginning of the collision with on-deck batter Dick Dietz and coach Leo Durocher cheering Rose home. The play was vintage Rose.

A mainstay of hockey arenas and ice rinks since 1949, the Zamboni machine finally had its outdoor debut in the 1960s with the development of artificial turf for places like the Astrodome, Three Rivers Stadium, and of course, Riverfront Stadium. For baseball games, the ice-resurfacing machine first built by Frank Zamboni's family plant in California was redesigned to become a giant suction device to remove water from the field, and was called the Astro Zamboni. Able to cruise at a top speed of nine miles per hour, each Zamboni was hand-assembled, and more than 7,000 ice and water machines have been built since that 1949 model. The first machine purchased for Riverfront, shown here in 1972, was Model ATZ #105. Two years later, a second Zamboni, Model 109, was added. The Zamboni machine also had a distinct economic effect. By helping to eliminate rainout games that would need to be rescheduled as double-headers, revenue for tickets, parking, and concessions would be far more for the regularly scheduled number of games.

Like the new stadiums in other cities—Atlanta, Pittsburgh, St. Louis, Philadelphia—Riverfront Stadium was in many ways an architectural response to the cultural upheaval of the 1960s. Built in a saucer shape and carpeted with permanent grass—Astroturf—the stadiums were situated in concrete islands with easy access by interstate. Fans could drive into town in isolation, park at the stadium and see a game, and drive home again without ever coming into contact with a turbulent and ever-changing urban environment. It felt safe. And, as the numbers show, it was what fans wanted.

a million thanks—
make that two million thanks, fans, for a great season!!!

1970 home attendance:

crosley field	567,937
riverfront stadium	1,235,631
championship series game	40,538
world series	103,062
straight-A & future reds fans	147,723
	2,094,891

you're tremendous!!!
...from the cincinnati reds officers, directors, staff and players.

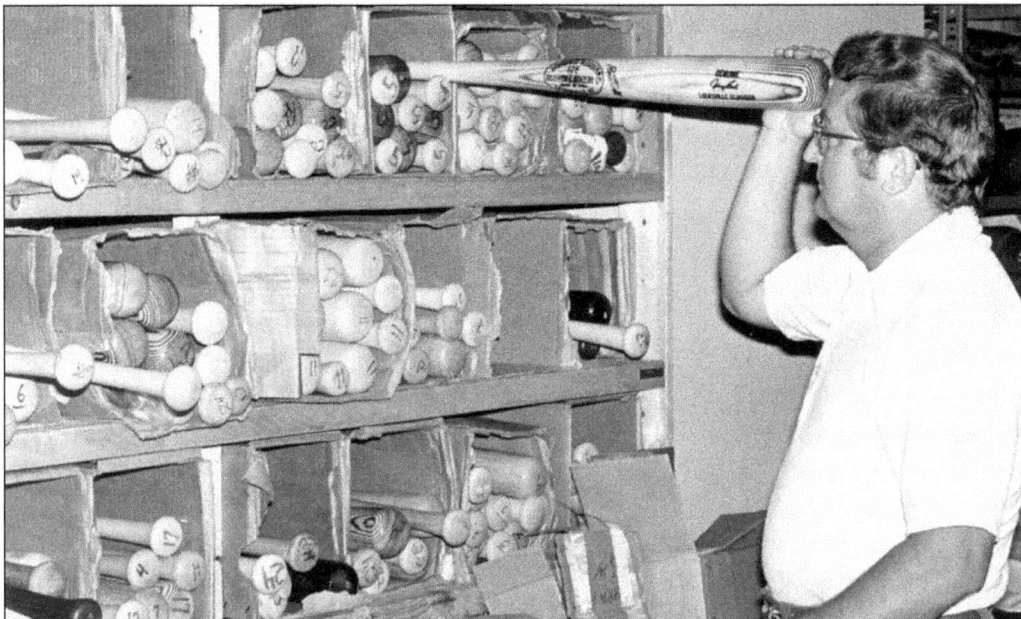

Bernie Stowe began working in the Reds clubhouse in 1947, when he was just eleven years old, and 55 years later he is still on the job. Tending to equipment and clubhouse duties became a family affair when Stowe was joined by his sons, Mark in 1975 and Rick in 1981. In Stowe's time, he has been a part of five pennant winners and three world championships.

A Cincinnati institution himself, first at Crosley Field and then at Riverfront Stadium, Peanut Jim Shelton hawked peanuts at ballgames for over fifty years. Wearing his trademark stovepipe hat, Peanut Jim sold his wares from his "Cadillac" pushcarts. He is shown here in a General Hospital room as he recovered from an illness on his 90th birthday in 1979, surrounded by nurses who honored the man's style. Shelton died in 1982 at the age of 93, and a stadium walkway was named in his honor.

George "Sparky" Anderson was named the Reds manager in 1970, just in time to lead them to their new field at Riverfront and into the World Series. Known also as "Captain Hook" for his quickness in yanking starting pitchers and calling in relievers, Anderson managed the Reds through the 1978 season, winning the world championship in 1975 and 1976.

With a powerful swing of the bat, Johnny Bench tagged a three-run homer against the Houston Astros on June 24, sending the Reds into first place to stay in the 1972 NL Western Division race with a 7–1 victory. Bench's home run, which curved into the left field foul screen, brought Rose and Joe Morgan around to score.

In another 1972 game against the Astros, Rose swings through a pitch. It didn't happen much that year. Rose struck out only 46 times in a league-leading 645 at bats and hit for a .307 average. Called by one writer the "quintessential Cincinnati Dutchman," Rose was Cincinnati born and bred. Even with his gambling scandal in the 1980s, it was tough to dismiss a local hero.

The Reds easily won the Western Division that year, and then beat the Eastern champion Pittsburgh Pirates in a close five-game NL championship series to meet the Oakland A's in the World Series. In this photo from a June game against the Phillies, Joe Morgan slides home after a sacrifice fly off the bat of Pete Rose. A Johnny Bench home run cinched the 2–1 victory. Bench would go on to capture his second Most Valuable Player Award

The Reds went up against the Oakland A's in the 1972 World Series, the first fall classic appearance for the A's franchise since 1931. The series started in Cincinnati, with the A's taking the opening game, 3–2. For the second game on October 15, baseball great Jackie Robinson was honored before the game at Riverfront Stadium and tossed out the first pitch. In this photo, the integration pioneer greets Oakland manager Dick Williams. The A's won the World Series, 4 games to 3. On October 24, two days after the Series finale, Jackie Robinson died at the age of 53. In 1997, the Reds joined the rest of the Major Leagues in permanently retiring Robinson's #42.

Another great player that graced the turf at Riverfront Stadium was the immortal Pirate outfielder, Roberto Clemente. On September 30, 1972, Clemente stroked his 3,000th hit at Three Rivers Stadium in Pittsburgh. On the last day of the year, he would die in an airplane crash while airlifting supplies to earthquake victims in Nicaragua. In this Cincinnati photo, Clemente crosses homeplate as a relay throw to Johnny Bench is off the mark.

Henry Aaron shows his joy as he kisses the baseball he smacked in the Crosley Field wall for his 3,000th hit. The historic shot occurred May 17, 1970 off Reds pitcher Wayne Simpson. St. Louis Hall of Famer Stan Musial is at his right and Braves owner Bill Bartholomay is at his left.

In this photo from a 1972 match-up between Cincinnati and Pittsburgh, Steeler quarterback Terry Bradshaw dances through the Bengal defense to score a touchdown for a 7–3 lead. The great quarterback could do little more that day, however, as the Bengals came back to win 15–10, all their points scored on field goals by kicker Horst Muhlmann.

In another game between the archrivals, a Bradshaw pass is headed for end Bob Adams, but bounced off his chest. Although the Bengals' defense couldn't quite handle the carom for an interception, the team did defeat Pittsburgh, 34–7.

118

From 1997 to 1982, Cincinnati was home to a professional softball team, the Cincinnati Suds (named for two Cincinnati institutions, beer and soap). Formed as part of the American Professional Slow-Pitch League, the Suds played their home games on the campus of what is now Cincinnati State College and, in 1978, they won the Central Division with a 40–24 mark. In 1980, a rival team, the Cincinnati Rivermen, was established as part of the North American Softball League. After that season, the two leagues merged, and then folded in 1982.

Known as the "Hawk" (What time is it? Hawk Time!), Cincinnatian Aaron Pryor won the junior welterweight crown on August 2, 1980. The bout against Antonio Cervantes was held in Cincinnati, and Pryor knocked him out in the 4th round. Pryor held versions of the title until 1986, when drug abuse ended his career. His exciting fights with Alexis Arguello in 1982 and 1983 are still discussed. In subsequent years, the Hall of Famer turned his life around to train his son and other boxers.

Jim Tarbell

CITY COUNCIL

VOTE NOVEMBER 4, 1997

As the decade of the 1990s came to a close, Cincinnati was once more caught up in a drive to build a baseball-only ballpark for the Reds and a stadium for the Bengals. One proposal, called Baseball at Broadway Commons, was for a ballpark in Over-the-Rhine between Broadway and Interstate 71. The plan was to make a neighborhood ballpark again. Its most vocal proponent was Cincinnati businessman, activist, and councilman Jim Tarbell. His 1997 election campaign even featured him on a baseball card, with his "stats" on the back. With Hamilton County voters already approving a sales tax hike to fund the new facilities, the question came down to where—Broadway Commons or the "Wedge," a site on the east side of Cinergy Field. By a two-to-one margin, county voters chose to stay on the riverfront.

THE NEW REDS BALLPARK AT BROADWAY COMMONS

View from Mount Adams

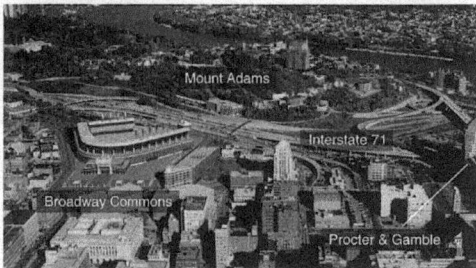

View from Carew Tower

View of Mount Auburn from Broadway

VOTE
YES!
on
ISSUE 11
NOV. 3

Paid for by Citizens for a County Charter for Baseball at Broadway, PAC. Bing Guckenheimer, Treasurer, 400 Reading Rd., Cincinnati, Ohio 45202

Six

INTO A NEW CENTURY OF ATHLETIC SPIRIT

2001–BEYOND

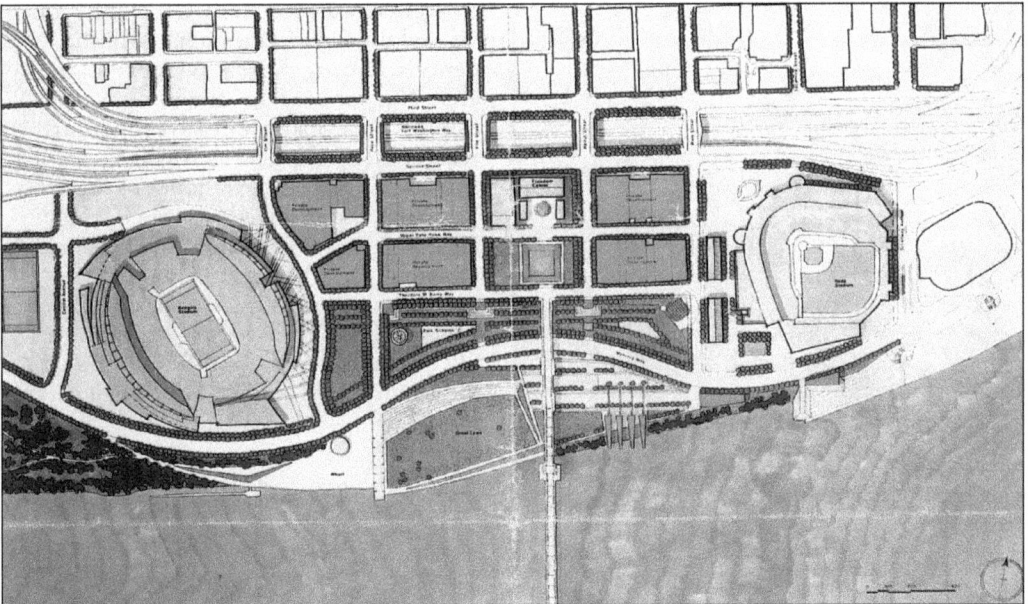

Getting ready for the new century, this plan submitted to the City of Cincinnati and the Hamilton County commissioners shows the re-design of the riverfront that would incorporate the new football and baseball stadiums. The Cincinnati Bengals would have a home in the futuristic-looking Paul Brown Stadium, while the Reds' Great American Ballpark to the east would incorporate more traditional elements in its architecture.

In 1968, Paul Brown and his investment group were awarded an NFL franchise and revived the old local team name of the Bengals. Playing the first two seasons in UC's Nippert Stadium, the Bengals moved to Riverfront Stadium in 1970, and thirty years later, on September 10, 2000, opened a new stadium named in honor of Brown. The Reds also prepared to leave Cinergy Field in 2001 (as Riverfront was renamed in 1996), with the construction on the Great American Ballpark to be completed in 2003. These photos show Paul Brown Stadium and a view down Walnut Street of the construction of the new baseball park.

In truth, Cincinnati has never been a major boxing town. In the 19th century, there were a number of bare-knuckle prizefights and amateur boxing matches at athletic clubs. In the 20th century, the city enjoyed for a while a regular slate of bouts at venues like armories, Redland Field, Music Hall, the old Parkway Arena, the Cincinnati Gardens, and small clubs dotted here and there in the core of the city. And, of course, Cincinnati has generated a few champions like Freddie Miller, Bud Smith, Ezzard Charles, and Aaron Pryor. But a small revival began in the 1990s, with local gyms training young boxers once more. One of the brightest stars to appear was Ricardo Williams Jr., who won a silver medal in the 2000 Olympics. After turning pro, Williams began his move up the junior welterweight ranks. The image shown here advertises a card he headlined at the Gardens in 2002. In a version of the sport closer to boxing as it was 150 years ago, the "Meanest Man" franchise attracts fans to small rings in rural parts of Hamilton County.

SUNDAY, FEBRUARY 24
THE CINCINNATI GARDENS
SUPER BRAWL SUNDAY

6-0, 5 KO'S

CINCINNATI'S OWN   2000 OLYMPIC SILVER MEDALLIST
RICARDO WILLIAMS, JR.
vs. ANTHONY WASHINGTON
10 ROUND JR. WELTERWEIGHT BOUT
DOORS OPEN: 1:00 PM/FIRST BOUT: 2:00 PM
TICKETS: $100, $60, $40, $25
CALL TICKETMASTER: 1-513-562-4949
OR VISIT THE CINCINNATI GARDENS BOX OFFICE
AT 2250 SEYMOUR AVENUE

The Meanest Man Contest
Is Back !

CALL NOW
242-1650
325-0715

30 FIGHTS
IN ONE NIGHT

The Greatest Boxing show Ever Produced !

FRI. FEB. 15 TH
2002

8:00 pm Strickers Grove, Rt. 128 Ross, Ohio
Please bring a can of good for the homeless.
Come rain, snow or ice-Be there !

Three weight classes   Giant Trophies-Plus
$1800.00 in prize Money- Ring Girls

$500.00 1ST
100.00 2ND
EACH WT.

For Information call 242-1650 — 325-0715

General admission $13.00

"Let me win. But if I cannot win, let me be brave in the attempt." The slogan of Special Olympics points the way for another category of athletes in Cincinnati and Hamilton County. As part of the national Special Olympics movement, the local program enfranchises citizens who normally would not be given a chance to participate and excel at sports. In the 2002 Spring Games held at suburban Lockland's high school stadium, events were held like the 50–meter and 100–meter dashes, wheelchair races, standing and running long jumps, the softball throw, and the shot put. More than 35 county agencies and schools took part, with more than 450 athletes competing. The 2002 motto said it all: "Inspire Greatness."

And the game goes on. Cincinnati playgrounds feed the passion for basketball, as do summer leagues, Midnight Basketball, and neighborhood driveways. One of the best runs in Cincinnati is at the Hartwell Recreation Center at the corner of Vine Street and Galbraith Road.

The current Cincinnati Ladyhawks are the second professional women's soccer team to play locally, preceded by the Cincinnati Leopards in 1995. Cincinnati also has a men's pro team in the Riverhawks, started in 1997. Previously, men's pro soccer had incarnations in the Comets (1972–1975), an indoor team called the Kids (1978–1979), the Cheetahs (1992–1993), and another indoor team called the Silverbacks in 1998 that played in the Cincinnati Gardens. In this June 2002 photo of the Ladyhawks, they move the ball upfield against the neighboring Northern Kentucky TC Stars, winning the game 2–0. (Photo courtesy of Joan Fenton.)

A recent manifestation of Cincinnati sports is the Dockers, an Australian Rules Football Club formed in 1996. On an oval field with a ball that is a cross between a football and a watermelon, the Dockers play an exciting sport that seems to combine basketball, football, soccer, and rugby. The Dockers are affiliated with the Fremantle Dockers in Australia, and in 1997 won the United States Australian Rules Football League national tournament.

Coming back from adversity or injury are characteristics in which Cincinnati sports fans place a great deal of stock. One player who personified that was Reds pitcher Jose Rijo. Rijo was the 1990 World Series Most Valuable Player in the team's sweep of the Oakland A's, but by 1995, his arm problems forced him into retirement. However, he never gave up. Six years and five surgeries later, Rijo was back on the mound on August 17, 2001. He pitched two scoreless innings to standing ovations from the fans, and he was back on the roster for 2002. (Courtesy of the Cincinnati Reds.)

126

BIBLIOGRAPHICAL ESSAY

Understanding sport in American culture supports a fuller understanding of everything else in national life, from industrialization and the building of cities to the heritage of immigration, from the role of politics and economics to literature and the infatuation with celebrities. A number of books eloquently and forcefully explore the shared context of sport and society. Among the best general surveys are Foster Rhea Dulles' *America Learns to Play: A History of Popular Recreation* (Englewood Cliffs, NJ, 1965), Benjamin G. Rader's exceptional *American Sports: From the Age of Folk Games to the Age of Televised Sports*, 4th ed. (Englewood Cliffs, NJ, 1999), John R. Betts' *America's Sporting Heritage, 1850-1950* (Reading, MA, 1974), and a very lucid examination by Steve A. Riess, *City Games: The Evolution of American Urban Society and the Rise of Sports* (Urbana, IL, 1989). Riess has also written a highly readable book, *Sport in Industrial America, 1850-1920* (Wheeling, IL, 1995) that continues the assertion of his work and of the others that it was urbanization and industrialization that gave rise to organized sport in America.

Two other books, while not about sport in particular, are of great help in relating the nature of athletics to American life: *Progressivism* by Arthur S. Link and Richard L. McCormick (Wheeling, IL, 1983) and *The Age of the Bachelor* by Howard P. Chudacoff (Princeton, NJ, 1999).

For the history of women in American sports, books worth examining are Sue Macy's *Winning Ways: A Photohistory of American Women in Sports* (New York, NY, 1996) and Susan K. Cahn's *Coming On Strong: Gender and Sexuality in Twentieth-Century Women's Sport* (Cambridge, MA, 1994). Cahn's book, particularly, takes a clear socio-cultural approach and relates women in sport to changes in women's status in society.

For understanding football in American society, some of the most insightful treatment can be found in *For Pride, Profit, and Patriarchy: Football and the Incorporation of American Cultural Values* by Gerald R. Gems (Lanham, MD, 2000) and *Reading Football: How the Popular Press Created an American Spectacle* by Michael Oriard (Chapel Hill, NC, 1993).

On baseball, the most comprehensive works are the three-volume histories written by Harold Seymour, *Baseball* (New York, NY, 1960, 1971, 1990) and David Q. Voigt's *American Baseball* (University Park, PA, 1993). Two single volumes on the sport are paragons on the placing of baseball in American society: *Our Game: An American Baseball History* by Charles C. Alexander (New York, NY, 1991) and Benjamin Rader's *Baseball: A History of America's Game*, 2nd ed. (Urbana, IL, 2002). On boxing, of note are Elliot J. Gorn's well-researched work, *The Manly Art: Bare-Knuckle Prize Fighting in America* (Ithaca, NY, 1986) and *Beyond the Ring: The Role of Boxing in American Society* by Jeffrey T. Sammons (Urbana, IL, 1988).

Charley Rosen's *Scandals of '51* (New York, NY, 1978) gives an excellent account of the college basketball gambling scandals.

Moving from the general to the specific, there are two excellent books on the early history of professional football in Ohio: Carl M. Becker's *Home and Away: The Rise and Fall of Professional Football on the Banks of the Ohio, 1919-1934* (Athens, OH, 1998) and *The Sunday Game: At the Dawn of Professional Football* by Keith McClellan (Akron, OH, 1998). Both volumes provide a good look at the development of football as an urban sport in Cincinnati, southwest Ohio, and the Midwest.

For Cincinnati, essential reading for understanding the city's development into the urban setting it is now – and thus, how sports would have been able to be seeded and grown – are Zane L. Miller's seminal urban history book, *Boss Cox's Cincinnati: Urban Politics in the Progressive Era* (New York, NY, 1968), and *Workers on the Edge: Work, Leisure, and Politics in Industrializing Cincinnati, 1788-1890* by Steven J. Ross (New York, NY, 1985).

Recent books on particular aspects of Cincinnati sport that are factually detailed are *From Club Court to Center Court: The Evolution of Professional Tennis in Cincinnati* ed. by Phillip S. Smith (Cincinnati, OH, 2001) and *The History of the Cincinnati Athletic Club, 1853-1976* by Jonathan Dembo (Cincinnati, OH, 1997). Thomas Nightingale's 1979 Ohio State University doctoral dissertation, *A History of Physical Education, Sport, Recreation, and Amusement in Cincinnati, Ohio in the Nineteenth Century* is a veritable catalog of early Cincinnati activities. A very interesting sidelight to local sports history, Tim Holian's *Over the Barrel: The Brewing History and Beer Culture of Cincinnati, Vol. 2* (St. Joseph, MO, 2001) discusses the relationship between Cincinnati sports and beer advertising and promotion.

For basketball in Cincinnati, see *Bearcats: The Story of Basketball at the University of Cincinnati*, a book I wrote along with Greg Hand, Carey Hoffman, Tom Hathaway, and Lisa Ventre (Louisville, KY, 1998). The book contains material on the early days of the sport in the city along with information on the current Bob Huggins era. Hathaway's media guides for the University of Cincinnati basketball program are models on how useful such books can be.

As one would expect, there is a wealth of books on the history of baseball in the Queen City. See my bibliography, *A Checklist of Books on Cincinnati Baseball* (Cincinnati, OH, 1994) for a compilation of writings, but there have been several excellent books written since this list's publication. The important books on Cincinnati baseball include Harry Ellard's early work, *Base Ball in Cincinnati* (Cincinnati, OH, 1907, reprinted in 1987) and *The Cincinnati Game* by Lonnie Wheeler and John Baskin (Wilmington, OH, 1988), the latter a thoroughly engrossing anecdotal account of the ins and outs of Cincinnati baseball history. Robert Walker's *Cincinnati and the Big Red Machine* (Bloomington, IN, 1988) provides a cultural/business look at how the Reds developed their success in the 1970s, and Michael Y. Sokolove's *Hustle: The Myth, Life, and Lies of Pete Rose* (New York, NY, 1990) gives a detailed look at the rise and fall of a Cincinnati sports icon. And, two indispensable books on learning about Cincinnati baseball are Gregory Rhodes' and John Erardi's *Crosley Field: The Illustrated History of a Classic Ballpark* (Cincinnati, OH, 1995) and *Redleg Journal: Year by Year and Day by Day with the Cincinnati Reds since 1866* by Rhodes and John Snyder (Cincinnati, OH, 2000), a book that is an incredible feat of research.

Recent video sports documentaries are also of great help: Donn Burrows' excellent *Flight of the Hawk: The Aaron Pryor Story* (1991), *Waite's World: The Life and Times of Waite Hoyt* (1997), and *The Big O: The Oscar Robertson Story* (2001); and Mark Watkins' illuminating *Safe at Home: Crosley Field and the Cincinnati Reds* (1995).

Visit us at
arcadiapublishing.com

....

www.ingramcontent.com/pod-product-compliance
Lightning Source LLC
Chambersburg PA
CBHW050652150426

42813CB00055B/1480